Presented to

Mama

By

Tensie

On the Occasion of

Mother's Day

Date

05/11/2003

WHEN GOD CALLS ME BLESSED

Devotional Thoughts for Women from the Beatitudes

ANITA CORRINE DONIHUE

BARBOUR BOOKS
An Imprint of Barbour Publishing, Inc.

WHEN GOD CALLS ME BLESSED

ISBN 1-58660-572-0

Published by Barbour Books, an imprint of Barbour Publishing, Inc., P.O. Box 719, Uhrichsville, Ohio 44683, www.barbourbooks.com

ecpa Member of the Evangelical Christian Publishers Association

Printed in the United States of America.
5 4 3 2 1

For ever, O LORD,
thy word is settled in heaven.
Thy faithfulness is unto all generations.

PSALM 119:89–90 KJV

Special gratitude and love to my aunt, Virginia Meitzler, for her love, guidance, and the personal example she has given me throughout my life.

Contents

INTRODUCTION

Blessed is the man
Who walks not in the counsel of the ungodly,
Nor stands in the path of sinners,
Nor sits in the seat of the scornful;
But his delight is in the law of the LORD*,*
And in His law he meditates day and night.
He shall be like a tree
Planted by the rivers of water,
That brings forth its fruit in its season,
Whose leaf also shall not wither;
And whatever he does shall prosper.

PSALM 1:1–3 NKJV

On a late February afternoon, I climb into my car and steer it toward a place of solace. I reach my destination: Flaming Geyser Park, near Auburn, Washington. Everything is quiet; it is still winter. Chilling breezes force me to zip my jacket and pull on my hat and gloves.

I leave the car and trudge up a small hill to the old geyser. Someone lit it today. Natural gas from beneath the ground feeds the flame. Now it only burns about a foot high. I've been told it used to be much bigger in years past. I wonder, *Will there come a time when its flame will die forever?*

After a few minutes, I start back down the path and walk toward the river. A trail to my right leads into the hills, where sometimes I hike with our sons. Good conversations take place on those walks.

I gaze across the recreation fields and recall numerous picnics and games we have had with family, church, and friends. I saunter farther down the path and reach the river where our family likes to wade. Once our church had a baptismal service in the lagoon.

Again I meet with God at the river's edge. He and I share good conversations there. Just God and me. Today will be one of those special times.

Trees line the shore. Some have no leaves. Their roots sink deeply, so they can drink continually from the pure, sweet water. Soon the sun will bring a warm spring. Tiny green buds will appear. During difficult times of illness or too much stress, my life is like that. In spite of hardship's chill, the Son of God's warm love manages to restore my joy and strength.

Whitecaps on the river move endlessly. They fill my ears with refreshing laughter. Brisk winds clear my mind of daily cares. Birds recently returned from the south send signals to one another, nestling into their protective bushy homes. Sunset nears. Soon wild animals will work their way to the water's edge to drink, then bed down for the night.

Everything is peaceful and orderly. I can imagine God's hands spread out over His masterpiece.

My prayer drifts on the breezes out over the water. *As much as You care about all of this, oh, God, how much more are You mindful of me, Your child.*

Nature in all its glory doesn't have a soul. It cannot worship You. We have the choice of following aimless paths of careless scoffers or sinking our roots deeply into Your Word. I could allow the flame You generously placed within me to fade to nothingness. Instead, I seek to fan Your flame into a powerful fire, never to die.

"I choose You, dear Lord," I call out loud and clear. "Through carefree or difficult times, I choose You, You from whom all blessings flow. I will follow You all the days of my life!"

* * *

May God bless you as you read this book. May you seek and find solace—even if it's only for an hour, a few minutes, or a few seconds.

May He bless you as you weave through the busyness around you and choose the quieter way. Perhaps it's time alone in the park. It may be taking the slower road home, instead of rushing on the freeway.

Breathe in deeply the winds of His holy presence. Feel Him fan the spiritual flame He carefully placed within you. Experience His power and strength as He causes the flame to steadily brighten —never to be extinguished.

May your conversations with Him be open as You share your joys, concerns, and sorrows. Take out your Bible and read God's priceless words of wisdom and sureness. Walk with the Lord down the path of righteousness. Pause and listen while He ministers to your soul.

Plunge into His exhilarating, living stream. Allow Him to wash away whatever may not be pleasing to Him. Drink. Be refreshed and strengthened deep within. Realize God's longing for you to have a future of immense joy and hope. Hear His words of love. Nestle into His protective arms, and be nourished by His love.

When we seek the Lord, He has an amazing way of calming our apprehensions and fears and of helping us set our lives in order. Step by step, day by day, obey the Lord.

May He spread His hands out over your life, grant you peace of heart, and bless you beyond measure.

Blessed Are. . .

THE POOR IN SPIRIT

And seeing the multitudes,
He went up on a mountain,
and when He was seated
His disciples came to Him.
Then He opened His mouth
and taught them, saying:
"Blessed are the poor in spirit,
For theirs is the kingdom of heaven."

MATTHEW 5:1–3 NKJV

Rich in the Lord

"My soul glorifies the Lord
and my spirit rejoices in God my Savior,
for he has been mindful
of the humble state of his servant."

Luke 1:46–48 NIV

When I first met seventy-year-old Daryl, I wondered if he were too good to be true. He entered the church wearing a red and blue plaid coat and a smile that never faded. No matter how bad things seemed, Daryl could recite a positive Scripture and turn the situation into praise for the Lord.

The Bible, of course, is his favorite source of knowledge and wisdom. He is also constantly striving to learn new things. To everyone's surprise, he speaks fluent Japanese.

God's house is truly his second home. He works very hard on local farms to make ends meet. For the time being, poor eyesight makes it impossible for Daryl to drive. If his work causes him to miss connections with his ride to church, he walks however many miles necessary in order to be there. No matter how tired and worn he is, Daryl bubbles with the joy of the Lord. Because of this, it didn't take long for me to realize Daryl was simply reflecting the glory of God. Jesus is Daryl's dearest love. He often shares how he was saved by God's rich grace. Whenever he's blessed, he laughs aloud, raises both hands, and says, "Glory be to God!" It isn't unusual during a sermon to glance over and see Daryl on his knees by his chair, praying. He has an unforgettable way of reflecting the Savior he adores.

Daryl doesn't seem concerned about looking or sounding important. He has a humble way about him. He doesn't have much in earthly treasures, but he is spiritually rich. Daryl's awesome gift from God is his music.

At the beginning of the service, I marvel every time I see Daryl quietly slip up to the piano and start playing. His hands glide over the keys as naturally as breathing. His weather-browned face shows the solace he gains from playing for the Lord. Before long, he has our little sanctuary sounding like a cathedral. Then he sings. His baritone voice rings out like an angel's. I often sense the presence of the Lord with each note. At times, someone starts to sing a hymn or chorus without written music. Daryl catches the pitch and joins in on the piano.

After worship services, the children gather round him. Daryl gently guides them on the piano and in song. He spent many years teaching lessons on that treasured instrument, and he understands the young. Children know when an adult truly loves them and cares.

Daryl doesn't boast or try to please others. He has found one of God's most precious blessings: happiness given to one who is humble and poor in spirit.

Thank you, Daryl, for being you and for allowing God to use you to honor Him.

The art of being happy lies in
the power of extracting happiness
from common things.

Henry Ward Beecher, 1813–1887

Weak but Willing

He has showed you, O man, what is good.
And what does the Lord require of you?
To act justly and to love mercy
and to walk humbly with your God.

Micah 6:8 niv

It wasn't long after Dave earned his college degree that he felt God's call to the ministry. It came as a complete surprise. He was planning to become a high school teacher. Although Dave studied hard, he never held a four-point grade average. He was not blessed with any outstanding talents, and he could name numerous faults he struggled with. He could not even sing on key. How could he ever measure up to the perfect example he felt was required for a minister?

For the next several months Dave studied the Scriptures and asked God to help and lead him. The closer he drew to God through prayer and reading his Bible, the more he became aware of his weaknesses.

"Lord," Dave prayed, "show me how I could ever be the kind of minister You ask of me. I want to serve You, but I don't know how."

One morning Dave sat at the open kitchen window, deep in thought. Birds chirping caused him to glance outside at the birdfeeder. He noticed one feathered creature singing more beautifully than the others. The little bird enthusiastically puffed out its chest, and glorious melodies filled the air. Dave was surprised when he discovered the bird had a missing leg. Still, it shuffled about, appeared happy, and kept singing. Serendipity? Or was this God answering his prayer? Dave believed it was the latter.

"God, You must not care whether I am weak or strong—talented or average. I realize now I can be worth more to You by merely being a loyal servant. You have promised me in Your Bible that Your grace is sufficient for me, and Your power is made perfect in my weakness. I trust You will provide me with confidence, joy, and strength."

* * *

In spite of Dave's weaknesses, God honored his faith. Doors opened for Dave to become a youth minister, where he is still winning souls for the Lord.

The Poor in Heaven

In Christ's conception of the blessed life, I find mentioned many persons that I did not expect to find referred to, and I find many persons omitted that I expected would have been first referred to. Let me take the beatitudes as a picture of Heaven. Who is Heaven? Blessed are the mighty, for they are in Heaven; blessed are the rich, for theirs is the kingdom of glory; blessed are the famous, for theirs are the trumpets of eternity; blessed are the noble, for the angels are their servants. Why, that is not the text. Who is Heaven? The poor in spirit. Then, perhaps, we may be there. Not many mighty, not many noble, not many learned, not many brilliant are called; then perhaps we may be there. Woman, mother, sisters, obscure person, unknown life—you may be there.

Joseph Parker, D.D., 1830–1902

Thou Didst Leave Thy Throne

Thou didst leave Thy throne and Thy kingly crown
When Thou camest to earth for me;
But in Bethlehem's home was there found no
room
For Thy holy nativity.

O come to my heart, Lord Jesus!
There is room in my heart for Thee.

Heaven's arches rang when the angels sang,
Proclaiming Thy royal degree;
But lowly birth didst Thou come to earth,
And in great humility.

O come to my heart, Lord Jesus!
There is room in my heart for Thee.

The foxes found rest, and the birds their nest
In the shade of the forest tree;
But Thy couch was the sod, O Thou Son of God,
In the deserts of Galilee.

O come to my heart, Lord Jesus!
There is room in my heart for Thee.

Thou camest, O Lord, with the living Word
That should set Thy people free;
But with mocking scorn, and with crown of thorn,
They bore Thee to Calvary.

O come to my heart, Lord Jesus!
There is room in my heart for Thee.

EMILY E. S. ELLIOTT, 1836–1897

YOU ARE MY WORTH

He guides the humble in what is right
and teaches them his way.
All the ways of the LORD are loving and faithful
for those who keep the demands of his covenant.

PSALM 25:9–10 NIV

Father, it didn't seem that long ago when I was pouring out my insecurities and frustrations to You and asking You for help. How I thank You for taking compassion upon me. You brought me out of my fear of rejection.

Everything seemed to be going well, but now it's all out of balance. Where did I mess up, Lord? How did I get myself into this yo-yo lifestyle?

I was so haughty the other day toward that person, forgetting I was once in the same place. I'm ashamed, Lord. I know You don't want me to be a doormat, but I'm beginning to realize that my attitude is not of You. Please forgive me, and help me to ask forgiveness of the one I offended.

Why should I even want to brag or look down my nose at someone? My achievements and failures are in Your hands.

Whenever I have no confidence in my abilities, I frantically turn to You for strength and guidance. Then when my self-worth grows, I'm tempted to become overconfident. It doesn't take much for me to charge zealously ahead and take everything into my own hands. That's about the time You allow me to take a fall.

In my distress I call upon You. Help me through this problem I have caused, Lord. Thank You for hearing my contrite prayer. Lead me, I pray. Help me to do what is kind, fair, and right.

I love You, Lord. *You* are my sureness and security. You are my counselor and guide. From You comes all wisdom and discernment. In You I find refuge and complete focus.

To those who are faithful, I see You make known Your faithfulness. To the humble, You show Your tenderness. Any worth I have comes from You.

Now I bow before You, Lord, and ask You to rescue me from my unkind thoughts and ways. Thank You for humbling me and once again bringing me back to Your will.

Teach and guide me in all that is right. Show me Your loving and empathetic ways. Grant me grace, and let me pass that grace on to others.

Give me the faith, I pray, to trust in You with every fiber of my being. Remind me not to depend entirely upon my own understanding. In every single way I will acknowledge You, so You can help me along the right paths.

I will not be wise in my own eyes. Instead, I will fear You, Lord, and turn away from haughtiness and evil. As I remain within Your will, I thank You for providing me with love, joy, peace, and self-worth and for making me Your child. In Jesus' name, amen.

Blessed Are. . .

Those Who Mourn

"Blessed are those who mourn,

For they shall be comforted."

Matthew 5:4 NKJV

Ann's Blessing

"I will never leave you nor forsake you."

Joshua 1:5 niv

It was Christmastime. Twenty-six-year-old Ann and her husband Bruce were finally expecting their first child. Ann had been praying for six years that she would become pregnant. Now, she and her sister were expecting babies at the same time. They were two and one-half months along. Both were thrilled and could hardly wait for their new arrivals.

The next time Ann went to her doctor, she was told something was terribly wrong. The baby wasn't developing right. The little one would be seriously disabled and possibly suffer from a life of misery. The doctor predicted Ann would lose her baby in the next few days. He tried to prepare her as much as possible. He even warned her she would most likely blame someone for her loss.

Ann prayed and prayed for God to help her keep her baby. Two weeks passed. Sadly, she miscarried. She remembered her doctor's warning about blame. She refused to blame Bruce or herself. Instead, Ann turned her bitterness toward God.

Bruce tried comforting her the best he could,

but nothing helped. For a long time, Ann was barely able to pray. Finally, she poured her heart out to the Lord.

"God," she sobbed, "why did You have to take my baby? You're a miracle-working God. You could have made everything okay. Why did You allow this to happen? Why?"

For about a year, Ann couldn't get past her anger with the Lord. She felt so alone in her grief. Finally, God was able to reach into her heart in an awesome way. He helped Ann realize her baby was happy and with Him in heaven. God wrapped her in His loving arms and comforted her through her mourning. Ann asked God to forgive her for her anger toward Him and thanked Him for His patience, mercy, and grace. She promised she would never blame God again. Even though she had felt alone, Ann now recognized God had been and was with her all the time. She recalled in her Bible how Jesus also experienced loneliness and grief. He really did understand. Little did she know, however, that she would experience two more miscarriages.

After her second miscarriage, Ann lost so much blood she almost died. She lay semiconscious in her hospital bed. Tormenting thoughts floated through her mind and would not go away. She fought them with all her mind and soul.

Jesus! she prayed.

Instantly, the torment stopped. *I know who I am, and I know* whose *I am!*

Ann felt God's peace and love saturate her mind and soul. She couldn't feel her body or hear anything. She could only communicate with her Lord. *Have I become a vegetable?* Ann wondered.

In spite of it all, she continued to feel God's presence. *God, please take me home. I don't want to be like this.*

At that moment, Ann rallied. She could hear the nurses. She felt cold. She knew she was going to live.

Ann learned a valuable lesson from her experience, one she wants everyone to know: "No matter what happens, no matter how far gone we are mentally or physically, God is still with us. He will never leave or forsake us. No matter where we go or what state we are in, He will be right there with us!"

Ann was glad to be alive. She felt stronger and able to leave everything with God. This time she didn't need to mourn. She knew her baby was with the Lord.

A little over a year later, Ann became pregnant again. She managed to reach five months into her pregnancy. She was starting to show and was experiencing a little life moving within her.

Ann began feeling sick. She called her doctor, and he sent her to the hospital. Infection had set in. The baby's heartbeat had stopped. Two days later, Ann lost a baby boy.

She wanted to have her tubes tied, but her husband encouraged her to wait. Perhaps there would be another chance.

One morning after church, a man in their congregation came up to Ann and told her God would restore the treasures of her heart, by giving her another baby. Ann wrote down the words, never to forget them. She would leave everything in God's hands.

Fifteen months later, Ann once again became pregnant. She was overjoyed and felt totally confident in the Lord. She felt she would have a baby boy. The doctors soon discovered Ann was expecting twins. Sadly, they could only get the heartbeat of one baby. One had died.

Tests were run. The doctors said her twin that was still alive would have Down's syndrome and other possible complications. The doctors asked Ann and Bruce if they wanted to terminate the pregnancy.

Bruce and Ann's answer was an emphatic "No!" They wanted their baby.

God continued to assure Ann He was with her and her baby every step of the way. Although the baby was due around August 16, the doctors anticipated the infant would be born a month early. Ann's regular doctor would be out of town during that time. She had been seen by several of the hospital's physicians and felt comfortable with any one of them delivering her baby.

While Ann sat on her front porch praying one morning, she sensed God talking to her heart. She felt Him asking her if she wanted her child born when her doctor was there or on her dad's birthday. Ann was ecstatic. She asked God to bring the baby on July 20, her dad's birthday.

Sure enough, Ann gave birth to a healthy, normal baby boy named Mitchell on July 20. God truly did restore Bruce and Ann's loss. The time of mourning was passed. The time of rejoicing had come.

Bruce and Ann continue to thank God for giving them a wonderful son. Mitchell is doing well. He's healthy, bright, and happy, and he loves the Lord. God truly blessed their family as He had promised He would.

Used by permission from

Ann

God Hath Not Promised Skies Always Blue

But God hath promised strength for the day,
Rest for the labor, light for the way,
Grace for the trials, help from above,
Unfailing sympathy, undying love.

Annie Johnson Flint, 1866–1932

Everything Lost, Everything Gained

"I have come that they may have life,
and that they may have it more abundantly."

John 10:10 NKJV

"I tell you the truth,
whoever hears my word and believes him
who sent me has eternal life
and will not be condemned;
he has crossed over from death to life."

John 5:24 NIV

Jill felt a hammer had hit her in the chest when she heard her father talking on the other end of the phone line. Dad was going to die? How could that be? He appeared so healthy, except for a pesky cough. He was the strong one in her life.

Jill's father, Phillip, had just returned from the doctor's office. Routine tests, they said. Nothing scary about that. After all, he was getting older. Yet the results came back with grim news. Her father had a fast-growing cancer that had spread throughout his body.

"I'll be right over, Dad." Jill could barely see through tear-filled eyes as she drove the short distance to her father's house. When Jill was a teenager, her mother had died in a car accident. Now this? It just couldn't be.

During the next few months, Jill remained as close to her dad as possible. Surgery. Chemotherapy. Radiation. Nothing helped. The disease continued to destroy her loved one.

What hurt most was when her dad wouldn't talk. It was like he didn't want her around. When he would allow her to see him, he would never discuss his condition. Was he attempting to block the whole thing out? Sometimes when she came over, he just turned his back, as though he were in his own world.

Weeks later, he seemed angry with her and everyone around him. He especially lashed out at the doctors. Although his behavior hurt her deeply, Jill wouldn't give up on loving him.

Father and daughter grasped at straws. Could there be a miraculous cure? Surely there was something they could do.

The thing that concerned Jill the most was her dad never gave any indication he had asked Jesus into his heart. Jill loved the Lord and felt this was the most important thing in a person's life. She had been praying for him for years. Now she prayed even harder.

While waiting between treatments in the hospital, Jill felt God urge her to talk with her father once more about the Lord.

"Dad—" Jill paused. "Have you ever asked Jesus into your heart?"

Her father shook his head.

"Dad, God loves you so much that He gave His Son for you. I want you to know Him as your Savior. I want you to experience His love. Dad, I really want to be able to be with you in heaven someday.

"Would you like to ask Him to become your Savior?" Jill held her breath and waited for his response.

Her father nodded. They took hands and prayed. First Jill prayed. Then her father—in his own halting, simple way—asked Jesus to forgive him and to come into his life.

Thus began the journey of Jill's father, Phillip. Jill watched him go through the changes from holding tightly on to everything here on earth, to looking forward to everything in heaven.

She knew her father had started a journal. He told her it would be something he could leave that she would treasure. Jill often wondered what he was writing, but she never invaded his privacy. The most treasured times father and daughter had together were spent recalling special memories. Best of all, however, was when they read God's Word. Frequently, her pastor came by and they all prayed together. Each time Jill read from the Bible's precious promises, she noticed her father close his eyes. A peace came over his face she had never seen before.

One day Phillip asked his daughter to make arrangements for him to be baptized. Their pastor reserved the church sanctuary for a Sunday night.

The night arrived. A handful of close friends joined them. The pastor stepped forward and said a few words. Jill could feel a renewed strength in her father as she helped him to the baptistery.

The pastor raised one hand. The other arm steadied Phillip. "I baptize you in the name of the Father and the Son and the Holy Ghost."

When Phillip came out of the water, Jill gasped. Her precious dad glowed. The man who was normally quiet and not much for words talked for two or three minutes about how thankful he was to be a child of God. This was a healing moment for Jill and her dad.

Phillip got to the point where he wasn't strong enough to write in his journal, so he asked Jill to write for him. First, he instructed her to read what he had already written.

The mysteries of her dad's previous actions were revealed. He explained how he couldn't believe, or didn't want to acknowledge the fact, that he would die.

What would happen to Jill and his dearest friends? How he longed to make things right with a brother he hadn't seen in years. His heart was breaking that he wouldn't be able to be there when Jill someday married, and he would miss out on the experience of having grandchildren.

Jill read on. She began to realize her dad had been grieving. Not only for what his daughter was going through, but for himself. She had been so caught up in her own hurt she didn't understand until now. She would be losing her dad. Her father would be losing his daughter, his friends, his familiar surroundings. He would be leaving it all.

Each time Phillip was strong enough to dictate, Jill wrote his feelings in the journal: treasured memories and thoughts; a letter to his brother; one to the man his daughter would marry; and another to his future grandchildren. He hoped to meet them in heaven someday.

Jill talked her dad into letting her call his brother. Fearfully, he agreed. The two reunited with tears and forgiveness.

During the last few weeks of Phillip's life, Jill watched her dad let go of everything present. It was like he was being ushered into a personal closeness with God.

Jill sat near her father when he was about to die. She softly stroked his hand and whispered a prayer near his ear. "Jesus, take good care of my dad. I know he's in capable hands with You."

She sighed and went on. "It's okay, Dad. You can go be with the Lord now. I'm all right. I know your love and the love of Jesus will never leave me—and Dad, I love you, too."

* * *

Jill had a peace in her heart after her father passed away. She was thankful God helped them both through their grief and the valley of the shadow of death. Now her father had everything, in Jesus Christ.

When We All Get to Heaven

Sing the wondrous love of Jesus,
Sing His mercy and His grace;
In the mansions bright and blessed,
He'll prepare for us a place.

While we walk the pilgrim pathway,
Clouds will overspread the sky;
But when trav'ling days are over,
Not a shadow, not a sigh.

Let us then be true and faithful,
Trusting, serving every day;
Just one glimpse of Him in glory
Will the toils of life repay.

Onward to the prize before us!
Soon His beauty we'll behold;
Soon the pearly gates will open—
We shall tread the streets of gold.

When we all get to heaven,
What a day of rejoicing that will be!
When we all see Jesus,
We'll sing and shout the victory.

Eliza E. Hewitt, 1851–1920

I Know I Belong to You

For this reason I also suffer these things;
nevertheless I am not ashamed,
for I know whom I have believed
and am persuaded that He is able
to keep what I have committed
to Him until that Day.

2 Timothy 1:12 NKJV

How can this loss be happening to me, Lord? My heart aches deep within. My whole being feels so crushed I can scarcely breathe. Why, Lord? Why did You allow this to happen?

For a long time I didn't want to believe it was true. So staggering is my loss, I can't comprehend it. One day everything was so good. The next, my whole world fell in.

You are my God. You created the world. You made me. You can do anything, Lord. You could have stopped this from happening. I am so angry at others. I'm especially upset with You. It isn't fair. I don't know how I can go on. I've cried until there are no more tears. I feel like my soul is shriveling to nothing. I can hardly even pray.

I know these feelings aren't of You, Lord, but I simply can't handle it all. How will I ever be able to see any reasoning to this? Please forgive me for being so angry. I pray You will help me through.

I do love You, Lord. I thank You for having broad shoulders when I struggle and lean on You. Comfort me, I pray, during my time of mourning. Help me to give my loss to You. Fill this gulf in my life with Your strengthening Holy Spirit.

Thank You for caring about me in my time of need and hearing my woeful cries and concerns. Thank You, too, for not allowing me to go through more than I can bear. Lord, I pray for You to restore in me the joy of Your salvation. Renew a right and happy spirit within me.

I read in Your Word how You mourned for lost ones. You even grieved for Yourself, when You prayed in the Garden of Gethsemane and asked that God, Your Father, would take from You the horrible things to come. Not only were You to die like a criminal, You were destined to take the sins of the entire world for all eternity upon Yourself. How dreadful it must have been to anticipate such a horrible thing.

I am awed at how much love You showed by praying for the one who betrayed You and those who were about to arrest and kill You. I'm overwhelmed at how You prayed for everyone throughout time. You even prayed for me.

The finality of death shakes me to the core. Surely You are greater than the evil one who seeks to devour every soul. Lord, at this moment I commend myself and those I love to Your faithful care.

* I don't understand why things happen. But I know, Lord Jesus, *I belong to You.* No one can snatch me away from Your tender love as long as I believe in You. I am Your child, and You are my heavenly Father.

Wrap me in Your tender arms, I pray. Comfort and heal me. I trust You never to abandon me, even to the grave. You have promised to make Your path known to me. You, Lord, already have a plan for my future.

Thank You for allowing me to rest securely in You. Thank You for going before and behind me, for being on my right hand and left. You have told me there is a time for everything; there is a season for every activity under heaven. I realize there's a time to be born and a time to die. Through all this, I praise You for Your favor that lasts a lifetime—even a life eternal.

How I thank You for being with me while I weep through the night, and for helping me realize that rejoicing does come in the morning.

The flowers will appear on the earth once again,

and the time of the singing of the birds will come. (Song of Solomon 2:12 KJV, paraphrased.)

Thank You for helping me cling to You, my rock and my strength. Though I tremble, I shall not be destroyed. Though I shake, I shall not be removed from Your everlasting arms.

Thank You, Lord, for blessing me with Your comfort and faithful presence. Thank You as You lead me on to a way everlasting. In Jesus' name, amen.

Then cometh Jesus with them unto
a place called Gethsemane,
and saith unto the disciples,
Sit ye here, while I go and pray yonder. . . .
Then saith he unto them,
My soul is exceeding sorrowful, even unto death:
tarry ye here, and watch with me.
And he went a little further,
and fell on his face, and prayed, saying,
O my Father, if it be possible,
let this cup pass from me:
nevertheless not as I will, but as thou wilt.

Matthew 26:36, 38–39 KJV

These words spake Jesus,
and lifted up his eyes to heaven, and said,
Father, the hour is come;
glorify thy Son,
that thy Son also may glorify thee. . . .
Neither pray I for these alone,
but for them also which shall believe on me
through their word. . . . I in them,
and thou in me, that
they may be made perfect in one;
and that the world may know that
thou hast sent me, and hast loved them,
as thou hast loved me.

John 17:1, 20, 23 KJV

Blessed Are. . .

THE MEEK

"Blessed are the meek,
For they shall inherit the earth."

MATTHEW 5:5 NKJV

Patient Persistence

As a prisoner for the Lord, then,
I [Paul] urge you to live a life worthy of
the calling you have received.
Be completely humble and gentle;
be patient, bearing with one another in love.
Make every effort to keep the unity
of the Spirit through the bond of peace.

Ephesians 4:1–3 NIV

The tiny young lady in her midtwenties told a missionary society about her call from God to become a missionary in China. Their response was that she didn't meet the educational requirements. Not only that, she would never be able to learn the Chinese language.

In spite of their discouraging words, she listened only to the call God placed on her heart. Ever since she had become a Christian, she knew God was telling her to win souls in China. She knew she must listen to Him and go, despite what others said.

A few years later, the young lady bravely boarded a train destined to pass through Europe and Russia. She possessed a suitcase filled with cooking supplies, a sparse amount of food, and a rug to help keep her warm. Although she couldn't fathom what was ahead, she knew God would go before her.

After traveling by train, boat, and mule, she finally reached Yangcheng, nestled in the northern China mountains. God did go before her by linking her up with an elderly missionary woman who had already been serving in Yangcheng.

The young lady had no money left. She received no support from anyone in England. Fortunately, the older woman had managed to purchase an old house. She, too, had a dream and shared it with her new young friend. They would make the house into an inn. Each time the mule trains stopped there to rest and eat, the missionary women would tell the men Bible stories. God would provide the means to feed them.

That's exactly what they did. To start with, the young missionary fed the mules, while the elderly one told the mule riders Bible stories. One at a time, the two women won the roughhewn men to Jesus.

Sickness struck the older missionary. The

young woman learned how to run the inn and lead souls to the Lord before her elderly friend died. She was beginning to understand why God had called her to China. She was sent to take over the work the older missionary had started.

The new missionary kept her focus on God's calling—cooking, cleaning, and telling everyone who would listen about God. The work became increasingly difficult. Little money was coming in. She wondered how she would be able to continue financially. Did God have something else in mind? What should she do now? Again, she took her concerns to the Lord.

Not long after the missionary lady prayed, a high-ranking Chinese official accompanied by soldiers came to her for advice. The government had told the official that after many years, women were to stop binding their feet. Since the missionary was the only woman he knew with large feet, the official requested her to become a foot inspector. The government would pay her in money and food.

Still, the missionary woman didn't forget her calling. She would only inspect feet if she were allowed to tell people about the Lord Jesus everywhere she went. The official agreed.

The woman went from place to place inspecting feet during the day. At night, she gathered the people and told them Bible stories and of God's love. She continued this every place she went. Miraculously, the money she brought in was enough to keep the inn running.

This little missionary, Gladys Aylward, unwaveringly fulfilled God's call with patience and persistence. Instead of not being able to learn the Chinese language as she had been warned, she fluently spoke several different Chinese dialects. God used her to calm a prison riot and help bring about better prison conditions. She started an orphanage, cared for the wounded during World War II, helped bury the dead, and guided numerous orphaned children away from the war zone to safety.

From the time Gladys Aylward entered China until she went home to be with the Lord, God used her meek and patient persistence to reach out to countless Chinese people. Not only did she receive His spiritual blessings on earth, she inherited the kingdom of God.

A Loving Touch

"Now that I, your Lord and Teacher,
have washed your feet,
you also should wash one another's feet.
I have set you an example that
you should do as I have done for you.
I tell you the truth,
no servant is greater than his master,
nor is a messenger greater than
the one who sent him.
Now that you know these things,
you will be blessed if you do them."

John 13:14–17 niv

It was the end of a long night's work on my job in a fast-food restaurant. Standing on concrete night after night had taken its toll. I was getting bone spurs in the bottom of each foot.

Our oldest son, Bob Jr., was visiting from out of town. When I arrived home, he was waiting up for me. I stepped through the living room door, sank to the couch, and kicked off my work shoes.

As Bob and I began visiting, he sat down beside me and took my feet in his hands. Ever so gently, he began massaging them. I recoiled at the mere thought of his touching my sweaty feet. He never paused but kept rubbing and listening to me tell about my night's work. I think that was one of the greatest acts of love I have ever experienced, one I will treasure and never forget.

Servant of Love

He [Jesus] got up from the meal,
took off his outer clothing,
and wrapped a towel around his waist.
After that, he poured water into a basin
and began to wash his disciples' feet,
drying them with the towel
that was wrapped around him.

John 13:4–5 niv

Confusion and anxiety filled the air of the upper guest room where Jesus and His disciples gathered.

They had just finished the Passover meal. The defector, Judas Iscariot, had gone to perform his act of destruction. Not only did Judas fall to temptation, most of the other disciples would soon desert Jesus. Yet in spite of their lack of understanding and dedication, Jesus loved each of them.

Jesus got up from His meal, removed His outer garment, and wrapped a towel around His waist. Quietly, deliberately, He poured water into a basin and began washing each disciple's feet, then drying them with the towel. He was not only performing a humble task; he was doing the job of the lowliest of servants. Surely the disciples were too shocked to even speak.

Jesus came to Peter.

Peter said to Him,
"Lord, are You washing my feet?"
Jesus answered and said to him,
"What I am doing you do not understand now,
but you will know after this."
Peter said to Him, "You shall never wash my feet!"
Jesus answered him,
"If I do not wash you, you have no part with Me."
Simon Peter said to Him,

"Lord, not my feet only,
but also my hands and my head!"

John 13:6–10 NKJV

This loving act of Jesus cleansing His disciples physically and spiritually is beyond human comprehension. The King of Kings and Lord of Lords knelt there in total love and servanthood, washing dirty, sweaty, unworthy feet. This was only the beginning of all He did for His disciples—and for us as well.

No amount of service on our part can ever compare with His selfless acts of love.

He does most in God's great world
who does his best in his own little world.

Thomas Jefferson, 1743–1826

O Master, Let Me Walk with Thee

O Master, let me walk with Thee
In lowly paths of service free;
Tell me Thy secret; help me bear
The strain of toil, the fret of care.

Help me the slow of heart to move
By some clear, winning word of love;
Teach me the wayward feet to stay,
And guide them in the homeward way.

Teach me Thy patience; still with Thee
In closer, dearer company,
In work that keeps faith sweet and strong,
In trust that triumphs over wrong.

In hope that sends a shining ray
Far down the future's broad'ning way;
In peace that only Thou canst give,
With Thee, O Master, let me live. Amen.

Washington Gladden, 1836–1918

Too Good for Service?

Then he called the crowd to him
along with his disciples and said:
"If anyone would come after me,
he must deny himself and take up
his cross and follow me.
For whoever wants to save his life will lose it,
but whoever loses his life for me
and for the gospel will save it.
What good is it for a man to gain the whole world,
yet forfeit his soul?
Or what can a man give in exchange for his soul?"

Mark 8:34–37 niv

Father, so many times I long to take the easy road of life. I want everything to be predictable and in order. This is why I'm having so much trouble with what You are asking me to do. It is definitely outside my comfort zone.

I don't mean to complain, Father, but I'm not very good at this sort of thing. Why me? Couldn't You give this work to that nice person in our church who would do it so well? The very thought of my taking on this project makes me cringe.

I know this isn't the way You want me to feel. Please forgive me for my first reaction regarding Your request, Father. I recognize I must be willing to do anything in accordance with Your will. There must be a reason why You have asked this of me. Is this responsibility meant to teach me something? Or is it for the benefit of another? How can I complain about being inconvenienced after all You have done for me? I'm so sorry, Lord.

I read in Your Word how important it is to always be open to Your leading, whether it is "in season or out of season"—convenient or not. Help me be open to You in heart and mind. Teach me patience. Fill me with love, compassion, and understanding.

You open my eyes to the urgency of obeying You when I realize there may not be a second chance for me to accomplish what You want me to do. Your ways must become mine.

Caution me to keep my head in this situation. Help me, Father, to be willing to endure hardship and to keep my attention on the calling You have for me.

When I am weak, please make me strong. When I am frustrated, calm my spirit. When I am tempted to become impatient, grant me patience. When I run out of love, pour through me Your love. Help me run this race I so much dread; keep my focus, Father, on Your goal.

Although I long to be with You in heaven someday, I don't think about the rewards Your Bible promises. I just want to be worthy of being Your servant. Thank You for Your Holy Spirit speaking to my heart. Thank You for showing me I'm never "too good" for any job You have for me to do. Most of all, Father, thank You for Your mercy and goodness and for loving me.

Blessed Are. . .

Those Who Hunger and Thirst for Righteousness

"Blessed are those who hunger

and thirst for righteousness,

For they shall be filled."

Matthew 5:6 NKJV

Two-Way Conversation

Shew me thy ways, O Lord;
teach me thy paths.
Lead me in thy truth, and teach me:
for thou art the God of my salvation;
on thee do I wait all the day.

Psalm 25:4–5 kjv

The most important times in our lives as Christians are when we go to God in prayer. Not hurried, but blocks of time when we can share our deepest feelings of joys and sorrows, victories and concerns with our dearest Friend, our Lord. The more we talk with Him, the more we know how He feels about all that's going on in our lives.

Can you imagine rushing through conversation with your husband or wife, your children or best friends, day after day? There would be no bond, only distance and discouragement. Neither are we able to have a closeness with God unless we really take time to talk.

It's tempting in this fast-paced world to hurry

through our prayer time the way we gobble breakfast or take morning vitamins. We must find time to savor the moments with God. Talk and talk some more. Laugh with Him about the funny events; cry on His shoulder about the things that break our hearts. We need to tell Him how much we love Him. He wants us to accept His love in return. What relief we feel when we ask the Lord to search our hearts for any attitudes that should not be there. What peace we experience when we turn such things over to Him and leave them at the foot of His cross.

It's important after this, not just to go on our way. There's more. The most precious time of all with God is yet to come. It's when we pause and listen. And listen. Then listen some more. Effective and fruitful prayer with God must be a two-way conversation.

When we are willing to do this, we are getting to know the heart of God. It is then He gives us the privilege of realizing what *He* is concerned about. Finally, after keenly tuning our ears to God in prayer, we are able to visualize the wonderful call He has for us to acknowledge. He may show it to us in bits and pieces, or we may see the marvelous plan He has for us all at once. Either way, we must be willing to obey. It is then He is able to use us to represent His voice, His hands, and His feet to reach out to others and spread His love and good news. That's what we as God's children are placed on this earth to do.

Jesus wants to be our best Friend. He wants us to sit with Him and listen. He invites us to walk and talk with Him. He urges us to follow Him, wherever and whenever He leads us. What a full, triumphant life we experience when we do so!

Getaway with God

And I—in righteousness
I will see your face; when I awake,
I will be satisfied with
seeing your likeness.

Psalm 17:15 niv

Our son and daughter-in-law, Dan and Stayci, live in a quiet area. They are surrounded by a few neighbors with homes nestled between trees overlooking Puget Sound, a Christian camp made for retreats, a bird sanctuary, and a pond.

A pasture and corral housing their horse and goat spread peacefully at the foot of their back upper deck. Even while our grandchildren busily play, the surroundings send out messages of tranquility.

Dan is a morning person like me. He has often told me the most beautiful time of day at their home is when the sun is rising. Peaceful. Birds everywhere. I found myself longing to witness it.

I finally decided to do something about my wish. I asked Dan and Stayci if I could spend the night, so I, too, could take in this beautiful time of day. The answer, of course, was yes.

The time finally arrived. I came home from teaching, packed my bag with odds and ends—the most important being my Bible, notebook, and pen. I gave my husband a good-bye kiss and headed for my adventure.

After a terrific evening together and a quick night's sleep, I awakened at 4:30. I was ready to enjoy a tranquil time with God. I shuffled into the kitchen, attempting not to make a sound. My nose immediately picked up the warm aroma of freshly brewed coffee Stayci had thoughtfully set the timer for the previous night. I filled my cup and slipped out the dining room door to the deck with my Bible, notebook, and a paper towel in hand. The full moon cast a silvery sheen upon everything, making the night almost as light as day. Before long, Dan joined me on the deck. He leaned up against the railing while I relaxed in a deck chair. We were able to have one of those rare times of quiet, sharing our concerns, dreams, and goals over steaming cups.

After awhile, Dan went downstairs to his office. Now I was alone with my thoughts—and God.

I spread out my materials and took a deep breath. It was so peaceful. Stars hung lazily in the sky. I felt as though I could raise my hand and take hold of a fistful of the sparkly diamonds. Nothing stirred except the horse and goat, grazing in the pasture. They glanced my way, seeming curious about my intrusion, then returned to munching on grass, quietly standing like statues. I prayed and thought and prayed some more. Sweet-smelling dew settled around me. My mind gradually cleared of the clutter that interfered with my reason for being there. I wiped the dew from the table and materials with my paper towel. I stood, stretched, and slipped inside for a second cup of coffee.

The moon bid adieu and faded. The sun silently crested and painted the eastern horizon with graduated shades of purple, blue, silver, and brilliant yellow. Its rays slivered through the trees of the bird sanctuary across the road, playing hide-and-seek with the shadows.

I took more of my thoughts to God. This time I was willing to open my heart and listen to what He might be trying to teach me.

"How I long for You to create a clean heart in me, Lord," I whispered. "Teach me from Your Word, I pray. Help me draw from Your wisdom."

The two-way conversation began as I read my Bible. *"Blessed are those who hunger and thirst for righteousness."*

I dried the table one more time and turned to a story in my Bible. I read about a sensitive eight-year-old boy named Josiah, who became king of the Israelites. His life inspired me, the way he did what was right in God's sight.

The rising sun wrapped my shoulders with a blanket of warmth and caressed the muscles on the back of my neck. At the same time, I sensed God's presence wrapping my heart with warm love, security, and peace.

Trees exploded with birds. Hundreds flocked through the air. They soared and dipped in perfect aerodynamic fashion, as though they were performing daily drills. Without hesitation, they followed their leaders—propelling through the air, floating, then gliding to nearby trees and rooftops. Over and over they repeated their ritual. Finally, the multitude of fowl settled here and there, finding their morning meals God had provided. Some rustled through bushes and trees, gently chirruping to their young and giving them breakfast. Barn swallows went about their duties to their nested offspring, expertly zooming in and out of the open stable windows and doors, like skillful air force pilots taking off and landing.

How did they become so accomplished? Was it from hours of practice? Could it be by heeding the lessons of those with experience? Or both?

"This is the answer You are trying to show me, Lord," I whispered. "To hunger and thirst for what is pleasing to You. Let me be obedient and glorify You in all areas of my life."

I realized I must search and listen with an open heart. I must follow God's lead and heed the words of wise people. I must apply what I learn to my life and put to practice God's priceless lessons.

I bowed my head, acknowledging the Author of the beauty that surrounded me. My decision making, goals, wants, and desires were coming into focus, in accordance with His will. At that very moment, I could feel His Spirit fill and nurture my thirsty soul. I knew He was providing me with the righteousness, love, and wisdom I searched for.

Each day as I return to God and seek His will, I enjoy a fresh, new, strengthening fellowship with Him. Then I am truly blessed.

TO WHOM DOES RIGHTEOUSNESS BELONG?

But when the kindness and love of
God our Savior appeared, he saved us,
not because of righteous things we had done,
but because of his mercy.

TITUS 3:4–5 NIV

Righteousness and wisdom are often gained by years of experience in the school of hard knocks. Foremost, they are found by hungering and thirsting for the unfailing lessons of God found in His Bible.

Are righteousness and wisdom reserved only

for the elderly? Many times, we would say yes. However, this isn't always the case. We see older people who make wise choices, and we don't fear using their lives as examples to follow. Unfortunately, there are others who no longer seek wise advice or think discerningly within God's will. Sometimes they suffer sad consequences.

What about the young? How many times have you seen or heard the pure and perceptive words of children, teenagers, or young adults who truly love the Lord with all their hearts? I have, more than I can count.

I was astounded when I read in the Bible about Josiah. He became king of the Israelites when he was only eight. How could he at such a young age have been able to make important decisions required of a king? The Bible says, even then, Josiah did what was right in God's sight. Obviously, He listened to the advice given by those who loved God. At age sixteen, he sincerely sought the will of the God of his ancestor, David.

By the time Josiah turned twenty, he was purging Judah and Jerusalem of its idols. When he was twenty-six, the young king began cleansing the temple of all unrighteous things, then cleaning and repairing the precious house of God. All the days of his life, Josiah loved and served the

Lord. What wonderful things he accomplished by simply being obedient to God. Certainly, the Lord had filled him with righteousness, wisdom, and love.

I believe righteousness and wisdom are not dependent upon age. Instead, they are found by anyone who seeks the right and wise way with an open heart and cautious mind.

When making important decisions, we must remember to look for advice from discerning, respectful, God-fearing people, young or old, not the people we know will reinforce our preconceived ideas. Most of all, we must always hunger and thirst for the righteousness of God and not compromise our standards. Stepping outside of God's will in the slightest can spell heartache and disaster. When we do obey God, He will fill us to overflowing. This will happen, no matter our age.

One of my favorite Scriptures when I'm trying to make important decisions is: "But seek first his kingdom and his righteousness, and all these things will be given to you as well" (Matthew 6:33 NIV).

In our process of asking, God gives us answers. As we seek His will, He helps us find the right way. When we knock, in search of His guidance, God will most certainly open the door to right choices and wisdom. Then He will immeasurably bless us with peace and everlasting joy.

* * *

More important than where we stand
on the issues of life is what we are doing
with the time on earth we have been given.

Take Thou My Hand

Take Thou my hand, and lead me—
Choose Thou my way!
"Not as I will," O Father, teach me to say.

What though the storms may gather,
Thou knowest best;
Safe in Thy holy keeping, there would I rest.

Take Thou my hand, and lead me—Lord,
I am Thine!
Fill with Thy Holy Spirit, this heart of mine:

Then in the hour of trial
Strong shall I be—
Ready to do, or suffer, dear Lord, for Thee.

Take Thou my hand; and lead me, Lord,
as I go:
Into Thy perfect image, help me to grow,

Still in Thine own pavilion
Shelter Thou me;
Keep me, O Father, keep me, close, close to Thee!

Julia Sterling, late 1800s,
Ira D. Sankey, late 1800s

Fill Me, Lord

I will take the cup of salvation,
And call upon the name of the Lord.

Psalm 116:13 NKJV

Father, I am faced with another dilemma; I really don't know which way to turn. All the experience and knowledge I possess do not seem to matter for anything right now. My heart is racing, and my emotions churn in horrible turmoil. I want to do what is right, but I'm not sure what right is! I've gone to those I respect the most and have received a variety of opinions. I am at a loss as to what I should do. Please help me, Lord. Calm my spirit, and show me the way.

I come before You with an open heart, seeking Your will. Although I long for a quick and easy solution to this problem, I know You can see the whole picture. How I yearn for You to teach me Your righteous way and grant me Your wisdom.

I know You can see the future as You guide me, and I thank You for that. As I read Your Word, I feel my mind clear. Ever so slowly, things fall into place.

How blessed I am in seeking only the counsel of those who love and serve You. How I delight in Your love and guidance and want to meditate on Your teachings day and night.

Even though all seems uncertain and the difficulties of life surround me, I will sink my roots deeply into Your streams of living water. When unsettled discord parches my soul, I will not wither, for You are with me.

As I seek first Your will, O God, I trust that all the wisdom and surety I need will be given to me. Thank You for helping and directing me. My heart interlocks with Your will. I praise You for bountifully filling my spiritual cup until it spills over to those around me.

Thank You for helping me focus on You and synchronize my thoughts with the directions I read in Your Word.

Peace, I feel You leave with me. Not the peace those who don't know You have to offer. No longer is my heart troubled; neither am I afraid. I believe in You and thank You for being with me, guarding, guiding me all the way.

Blessed Are. . .

THE MERCIFUL

"Blessed are the merciful,
For they shall obtain mercy."

MATTHEW 5:7 NKJV

Tapestries of Mercy

Blessed is he who has regard for the weak;
the Lord delivers him in times of trouble.

Psalm 41:1 niv

Life wasn't always easy when my aunt Virginia was a little girl. Because of this, her aunt Rosa and uncle Fred took Virginia and her brother in. The children were adopted and made part of their aunt and uncle's family. The Christian couple watched over and nourished Virginia and her brother, and loved them like their own. They took the children to church regularly and taught them about the things of the Lord.

When Virginia grew up and married, she passed on the mercies shown to her by taking in and loving all sorts of people. Sometimes she cared for children. She also unselfishly gave her love to the disabled and the bedridden elderly.

Recently, at a loved one's funeral, I visited with adults in two separate conversations, whom Aunt Virginia had once taken into her care. She and Uncle Theodore's door was always open. Extra plates were often set at their table.

My mother worked long hours during difficult financial times. It was then that I stayed with Aunt Virginia. I, too, was fortunate to be one who received her love and mercy. For four years, she passed to me the blessings she had received in her own childhood. Through action and word, Aunt Virginia shared the love of God.

How beautiful she looked with her radiant smile and olive skin. Although she was prematurely gray, her curly tresses looked like a silvery halo to me. Her loving actions said far more than any speeches. They introduced me to my personal Savior.

Now Aunt Virginia has reached the age of ninety-two. She moves more slowly and is showing her age. Yet she is as lovely inside as ever.

In different ways than Aunt Virginia, I now have the privilege of passing her precious, heartening gift to others, through love and encouragement.

Through His all-knowing, precise purpose, God weaves His mercies through one generation to the next, like colorful threads in a tapestry. Now He places the well-planned strands in my hands and those of my God-loving cousins. He uses us to weave the endless strands in and out of the lives of those we contact. May God direct us as we do.

Through the methodical motions of His Holy Spirit, I look for His compassion to carry on through future generations. Someday, in heaven, the tapestries of mercies God interlaces in our lives will come to full view. How big and magnificent they will be!

Just as there comes a warm sunbeam
into every cottage window, so comes a lovebeam
of God's care and pity for every separate need.

Nathaniel Hawthorne, 1804–1864

Small Act, Big Blessing

He who has mercy on the poor,
happy is he.

Proverbs 14:21 NKJV

Wendy, a full-time elementary teacher and mom, had just finished a busy day at school. She was anxious to get home to her husband and two daughters. A quick trip to the grocery store for an easy meal would do it.

She steered into the parking stall and grabbed

her purse. She climbed out of her car just in time to see a man who appeared homeless, asking for help from passing shoppers. Some folks quickly glanced away, half embarrassed. Others shook their heads. A few handed the needy man a little change. *Is this man truly destitute? Or does he simply require a quick fix or a drink? I wonder if he's a scammer. There are so many like that,* Wendy pondered.

A second glance helped answer her question. Near the man was an old parked car. Inside were a woman and several small children. It didn't take long for Wendy to make her decision. She knew she had to help.

While buying her groceries for her own family, she purchased another bag including some nonperishable items: bread, peanut butter, jelly, bananas, juice drinks, napkins, plastic eating utensils, and a bar of soap.

When she left the store, Wendy spotted the man and his family. She got into her car, drove over to where he stood, and handed the man the bag of groceries.

"Here, sir. Maybe this will help," she said with a smile.

Wendy pulled away, glancing in her rearview mirror. The woman was spreading peanut butter sandwiches as fast as she could, while the children excitedly bounced up and down on the car seats.

Tears came to Wendy's eyes. She tried to swallow the lump in her throat. How surprising that God would help her see their needs.

"Father, I promise to always be willing to help others in any way You direct," Wendy whispered. Take care of this family, I pray. Help the dad to find work and a home. Thank You for the warm feeling this gave me."

Now Wendy carries a few nonperishable things in her car, ready to help someone else. She receives a big blessing of joy in return for each small act of mercy.

The Outcast's Mercy

" 'Which of these three
do you think was a neighbor to
the man who fell into the hands of robbers?'
The expert in the law replied,
'The one who had mercy on him.'
Jesus told him, 'Go and do likewise.' "

Luke 10:36–37 NIV

What kinds of people do you cross paths with each day? Are they all warm, caring, happy Christians? Do you ever walk or drive past some who are offensive, undesirable, extremely poor, or even dangerous? How do you feel about them?

I love being around my Christian friends, especially those who are caring. Like many of us, I also come across people who are in a hurry and seemingly going nowhere. Unfortunately, some are rude. Some are prostitutes, facing certain disaster. Whenever I see the offensive, the homeless, and undesirable, my emotions go into turmoil.

When I worked my night job at a fast-food restaurant, I witnessed people of all ages holding down two and three jobs. Several lived in their cars. They struggled to save enough to pay the huge deposit necessary to get into an apartment. At times, numerous young people were forced to share small apartments in order to keep a roof over their heads.

Some managed to kick the drug and alcohol problems, return to school, and develop a successful career. What surprised me was when they did so, they were often plagued by people from their past. Hands outstretched, some from the past, continually asked for money to squander. The ones trying to get their lives together were forced to search for wisdom so they wouldn't lose all their earnings.

Although they cared about others, how could they ever get ahead? Would they need to move away? The answers I used to think I had suddenly didn't come so easily. Along with other caring people on my night job, I learned to become a good listener and relate. I saw many lives changed by doing so. Miracles happened. Drug dealers, gang members, and prostitutes found a better way and a dream for the future because of the Lord working in their lives.

Some accepted Christ as their Savior. Some are still considering it.

One night a group of gang members came through the drive-through. They wore their colors proudly. The air vibrated with possible danger. Offensive music blared on their car radio while they waited for their food. Fear often caused the employees to avoid eye contact in dangerous situations, politely serve their food, and get them on their way. Then we gave sighs of relief.

Yet there was something different this time. I noticed a teenager in the backseat of the gang members' car. He must have been only about fourteen. I could sense the Lord speaking to my heart. I paused at what I was doing and searched his steel-like eyes. Our gazes connected. I was able to look into his soul. Angry. Frightened.

Nothing else seemed to matter as we looked at

one another. Then I offered a warm, kind smile. His eyes widened. A perplexed look came over his face.

God, help him get to know You, I silently prayed.

I believe that was the beginning of a change for that young man's life. Even though I could do no more, I felt confident God would have the next Christian ready to take the microscopic seed I had planted and nurture it. The feeling was so strong, I won't be surprised if I see him someday in heaven.

In some situations, we can help. Other times, God requires us to simply do one extremely important thing—pray. Please don't forget to do so. You will one day be surprised to see how God has answered your prayers.

Who Had Mercy?

When asked by experts in the law who had mercy, Jesus told the following story:

There was a man traveling from Jerusalem to Jericho. Before he arrived at his destination, the man was brutally attacked by robbers. They stripped his clothing from him and beat him unmercifully. Then they took everything the man had and left him dying beside the road.

Footsteps heralded the approach of a priest. Instead of helping, the priest skirted the area. He even went so far as to cross over to the other side of the road. We don't know why. Perhaps he was hurrying to the temple. Maybe he didn't want to get his robes soiled.

A Levite came up to the suffering man. He, too, avoided the situation and crossed the road. He possibly didn't want to get involved.

A stranger happened by—a man looked down on by many because he was a Samaritan. When the Samaritan discovered the critically injured man lying by the roadside, he stopped. He didn't walk away. Instead, he went over and knelt by the bleeding man.

If the wounded man realized who was tending him, would he have refused help from the Samaritan? It is highly doubtful.

The Samaritan reached in his bag, pulled out oil and wine, and gently poured it on the man's wounds. Ever so carefully, he took pieces of cloth from his belongings and bandaged the injuries.

He hoisted the man onto his donkey and took him to the nearest inn, but the Samaritan didn't leave. He remained with the injured man for the night and cared for him.

The next day the Samaritan handed two silver coins to the innkeeper. " 'Look after him,' he said, 'and when I return, I will reimburse you for any extra expense you may have' " (Luke 10:35 NIV).

The expert in the law had to admit the Samaritan was indeed the one who showed mercy. The timeless words of Jesus still ring in our ears: " 'Go and do likewise' " (Luke 10:37 NIV).

From Every Stormy Wind That Blows

From every stormy wind that blows,
From every swelling tide of woes,
There is a calm, a sure retreat;
'Tis found beneath the mercy seat.

There is a scene where spirits blend,
Where friend holds fellowship with friend;
Though sundered far, by faith they meet
Around one common mercy seat.

Hugh Stowell, 1799–1865

On What Condition Mercy?

The Lord *is good;*
His mercy is everlasting,
And His truth endures
to all generations.

Psalm 100:5 NKJV

Father, when I see the sin, sickness, sadness, and destitution around me, I'm driven to frustration. Why is this happening? What can I do to help, Lord? I'm only one person.

I grieve over these things and hurt for the ones who suffer. Some are people who are victims of circumstances. However, I realize there are problems some folks bring on themselves. I become frustrated when I see someone not willing to take hold of ambition and responsibility for her life.

And what about those who steal and hurt and kill, Lord? Must I be merciful to them? If given another chance, would they do the same things again? Should they be allowed to do so, Lord? Should justice still be done? I simply can't comprehend it all. This is where I seek Your wisdom.

As much as I hate it, there are times I know You require me to make life-lasting decisions. I can only do so with Your help.

I know I'm not meant to solve all of life's problems. On what condition do I show mercy? Grant me love, discernment, and the ability to know Your will, I pray. Show me how to encourage others when they have given up. Help me to understand how they feel. Guide me to recognize when You want me to help and when You want me to gently steer them toward being able to help themselves. Make clear to me when I am to leave the whole thing to Your care.

I know we aren't supposed to allow ourselves to be mistreated. When people sin, justice must still be done. Still, You tell us to forgive as You have forgiven us. Grudges and hatred can consume our lives like a deadly cancer. I realize such things aren't of You. No matter what the case may be, Father, remind me to keep praying for those who have done wrong, that they will turn their hearts to You.

I think of when I have been in want. I recall so many problems I created for myself and others. Thank You for Your mercy and forgiveness. Thank You for forgiveness I've received from those I wronged.

How I praise You, Father, for Your goodness.

I'm grateful for Your mercy that endures for all time. When all seemed lost, You did mighty wonders in my life.

You are the One who made the heavens and the galaxies—the sun to shine by day and the moon by night. You are the One who placed the earth in space and puddled the waters upon it. And You are the same God who lovingly, mercifully cares about me and teaches me to be merciful to others.

Thank You, Father, for Your great love and Your mercy that endures forever.

Blessed Are. . .

THE PURE IN HEART

"Blessed are the pure in heart,
For they shall see God."

MATTHEW 5:8 NKJV

The Unknown Artist

"Greater love has no one than this,
that he lay down his life for his friends."

John 15:13 NIV

It has been told he was born in the fifteenth century, most likely to a family that didn't have much money. During his growing-up years, he made a lifelong younger friend. His friend was one of eighteen children. Some say the two friends were brothers.

As they neared adulthood, the friends both developed a sincere love for art. The two young men became extremely talented. They longed to attend art school and pursue their lifelong dreams. Sadly, there were no means to do so.

The friends decided that one would labor for a number of years and help put the other through school. After the one completed his studies and became successful, he would, in turn, put the other through school. This way they would both be able to achieve their dreams.

It has been told the decision was made by a

toss of a coin. The loser went to work in the mines and helped pay for his friend's education.

Years went by as he labored for long hours, day in and day out. After his friend finished his studies and became successful, it came time for this caring man to have the chance to achieve his dream.

Tears probably filled the man's eyes when his friend came back from school to return the favor. Sadly, it was too late.

According to the story, hours of pounding and digging and pulling in the mines had caused numerous injuries to the unknown artist's hands. Every finger had been smashed, some broken at least once. Crippling arthritis had caused his once-nimble fingers to twist in response to constant pain. No longer could he even hold a brush or pen to the once-familiar canvas.

The reward of his labor may have been seeing his dear friend succeed. What greater gift could a friend have contributed.

The story passed down through centuries goes on to tell how the once-aspiring artist was seen by his friend kneeling one day—silently praying with hands clasped.

The unknown artist most likely didn't expect to receive the greatest heartfelt gift of gratitude possible from his friend, Albrecht Dürer—one of the world's most acclaimed artists: a sketch of the unknown artist's own broken, gnarled, love-filled praying hands.

The drawing became famous, later known as the treasured "Praying Hands." The heartfelt gift has been passed down through the centuries. Many of us are blessed by having a picture or carving of the well-known praying hands in our homes.

Some say "The Praying Hands" may have been a sketch of the hands of Albrecht Dürer's mother, or perhaps a replica of his own hands.

Whether this story of the unknown artist is true or not, the symbol of love attached to the praying hands reaches beyond friendship, beyond family, beyond giving of ourselves. It brings to mind the ultimate sacrifice our Lord Jesus gave because of His love for each one of us.

Pause for Prayer

Be joyful always; pray continually.

1 Thessalonians 5:16–17 NIV

And pray in the Spirit on all occasions
with all kinds of prayers and requests.
With this in mind, be alert
and always keep on praying
for all the saints.

Ephesians 6:18 NIV

A late summer night breeze unobtrusively entered the open front yard double French doors of Aunt Virginia and Uncle Theodore's old farmhouse. Mingled warm and cool currents wove their way between the dining room furniture, where our family had gathered. I knelt before a large wooden chair, my hands clasped, elbows propped on the sturdy seat, my eyes closed. The fresh air gently kissed my five-year-old cheeks.

My childish mind drifted back a few hours. In

the afternoon, rain had pelted outside our doors, followed by rattling pea-sized hail. My older cousin, Neil, had grabbed a kettle from the kitchen and ran out in the yard with it on his head. He said he wanted to get a full effect of the exciting rattle. Neil received a scolding when Aunt Virginia discovered multiple dents in the bottom of her pot while preparing supper.

The rain and hail settled the dust from a hot, dry spell. Welcome sounds of birdsongs and rustling tree leaves followed nature's clattering concert.

Now I could hear crickets harmonizing with frogs, accompanied by an occasional hoot from an owl. The air's sweet, clear fragrance recharged my sleepy mind.

My thoughts returned to why I was on my knees before the dining room chair. Other sounds registered—sounds I heard every night at bedtime during the four years I lived with my aunt and uncle: reverent, meaningful prayers that flowed upward from each family member. Adults and children alike were welcome to talk with God. We only paused for prayer for a few minutes, but it was a time to set things right before God and allow Him to touch our lives.

Soft, reverent voices worked their way around the room and drew closer to me. My "big" cousins,

Neil, Erma, Beverly, and my younger cousin, Steven, prayed.

My turn. "Dear God, I love You. Bless the birds. Bless the trees. Bless Aunt Virginia and Uncle Theodore. Bless my mother and daddy. Bless. . ."

* * *

Although nightly prayer in Aunt Virginia and Uncle Theodore's dining room didn't take long, the priceless memories linger for a lifetime.

My aunt's prayers for me and her Christian example led me through my childhood years and on into adulthood. Her advice was pure, simple, and filled with love. She gave me the best vision of Jesus I have ever known.

Aunt Virginia and Uncle Theodore's example of prayer at bedtime trickled down a generation, to my husband, Bob, and me. We began our marriage by praying together. It continued. We prayed with our children before school, during good times, trials, and almost always at bedtime. Praying together helped us avoid serious errors. When we did err, prayer guided us toward making things right. Prayer replaced strife with love and drew us closer to God and one another. After all these years, prayer still unites us as a grown extended family whenever we are able to be together.

In my personal life, communion with God begins with my rising in the morning. Bob and I pray together before we leave for work. I enjoy my treasured quiet prayer time alone in my recliner and my car. "Arrow prayers" shoot up from my desk at my job in the grocery store. Throughout the day, a two-way communication continues with my best Friend, the Lord Jesus. He remains by my side and guides my steps.

Uncle Theodore passed away a few years ago. Aunt Virginia is in a nearby nursing home; one or more family members see her almost every day. Her memory is beginning to fail; her energy ebbs. Still, when I sit by her, hold her hand, and talk with her about the Lord, her eyes light up and she smiles. She may have trouble recalling things, but she knows her Lord and Savior well. He is more than in her mind. His presence remains in her pure, yielding heart.

SPIRIT OF GOD, DESCEND UPON MY HEART

Spirit of God, descend upon my heart;
Wean it from earth; through all its pulses move;
Stoop to my weakness, mighty as Thou art,
And make me love Thee as I ought to love.

I ask no dream, no prophet ecstasies,
No sudden rending of the veil of clay,
No angel visitant, no opening skies;
But take the dimness of my soul away.

Hast Thou not bid me love Thee, God and King?
All, all Thine own, soul, heart, and strength
    and mind.
I see Thy cross; there teach my heart to cling;
O let me seek Thee, and O let me find!

Teach me to feel that Thou art always nigh;
Teach me the struggles of the soul to bear,
To check the rising doubt, the rebel sigh;
Teach me the patience of unanswered prayer.

Teach me to love Thee as Thine angels love,
One holy passion filling all my frame;
The baptism of the heaven descended Dove,
My heart an altar, and Thy love the flame.

GEORGE CROLY, 1780–1860

Purify My Heart

Create in me a clean heart, O God,
And renew a steadfast spirit within me.
Do not cast me away from Your presence,
And do not take Your Holy Spirit from me.
Restore to me the joy of Your salvation,
And uphold me by Your generous Spirit.

Psalm 51:10–12 NKJV

How can I ever have a pure heart, Father? Is such a thing possible? Again and again I fail. I start out the day the right way by coming to You in prayer. It's easy during this time. Just You, me, and my Bible. Then I'm forced to step out into the world.

The little things especially bewilder me, Father. Like the person who cut me off on the freeway this morning. I mumbled and spluttered and wanted to pass that car and flash a vengeful grin. Thank You for not allowing me to catch up. Help me, instead, to pray for safety for those crazy drivers and others around them.

There's the person at work, Father, who shares all the office gossip. I bristle every time I hear tongues wag. Yet I find myself listening to the destructive stories. What do my coworkers say about me when my back is turned? Help me avoid the gossip and be a blessing. Thank You for the good, caring people I work with.

The lady in the grocery store line really got to me, Lord. I was so tired and wanted to go home. I only had two little items in my hands. There I was in the express line. Ten items only, the sign stated. Funny. This woman ahead of me must not have been able to read, by the looks of her heaped-up basket. I wanted to help her count all those items, then cluck my tongue and wag my finger. I didn't, Father, but I know my attitude was bad. Please forgive me and help the woman sense Your love for her.

Coming home after a long day and facing my family without having a "kick the dog" mind-set was quite a challenge. Thank You for reminding me to take a deep breath and ask for Your loving strength before I entered the door and met the ones I love the most.

Father, I'm so frustrated. The things I want to do for You, I often fail to do. The things I hate, I find myself tempted to do. I want to have a pure heart, Lord, but I can't without Your help.

When everything is going just right, and I feel like I'm standing on firm ground, I find myself becoming lax in turning to You in prayer. It doesn't take long before the tempter sneaks in and creates confusion and turmoil. Help me stick close to You in the good times as well as the bad.

Purify my heart, O Father. Test me and try me. Probe my mind and soul. Reach in and sweep the cobwebs of anger, jealousy, malice, slander, and wrong thoughts and actions from my weary soul. Replace them with Your pure fragrance of compassion, empathy, and love. Cleanse me and fill me with Your Holy Spirit; I long to walk continually in Your sure way. Grant me Your strength, I pray, so my thoughts, words, and actions are pleasing to You.

I know whatever I think, so *am* I. Help me think on things that are true and noble, pure and lovely, admirable and praiseworthy. After these good things are planted in my mind, let me practice them in my everyday life. I pray for You to also instill them in my heart for now and eternity.

The next time the world crushes in and I become hurt, angry, or frustrated, help me remember to pause and pray. Dim my vision of the difficulties and temptations in this world, dear Father. Bring to light Your unfailing love. Thank You for providing victory over trouble and temptation. Thank You for empowering me to be more than a conqueror through You. In Jesus' name, amen.

Blessed Are. . .

THE PEACEMAKERS

"Blessed are the peacemakers,
For they shall be called sons [and daughters] of God."

MATTHEW 5:9 NKJV

The Peacemaker's Gift

"Peace I leave with you; my peace I give you.
I do not give to you as the world gives.
Do not let your hearts be troubled
and do not be afraid."

John 14:27 NIV

The child was only a baby when Moses bought him, his slave mother, and his brother Jim. Moses didn't care about the mother and children being slave workers. He simply wanted them to keep his wife Sarah company. Neighbors lived far apart and seldom saw one another. Soon Sarah and the baby's mother became good friends.

Moses didn't believe in slavery. He and his wife were pleased when freedom came to the slaves. By then, the baby was about one year old. No one knew for sure, because there were no records kept on the birth of slave babies back then.

Because of Moses and Sarah not believing in slavery and their acts of kindness, the baby's mother and family remained on the plantation after they were freed. Friendship between Sarah and the mother grew stronger than ever.

In spite of slaves gaining their freedom, the Ku Klux Klan didn't approve of Sarah and the mother's friendship. One night the Klan stormed Moses and Sarah's farm. Moses saw them coming. He quickly grabbed Jim and hid him. But before he had a chance to rescue the others, the Ku Klux Klan took the mother and baby away.

As soon as morning came, Moses searched for the mother and child. Only the baby could be found. The mother was never to be seen again. Moses and Sarah took care of the baby and his brother. For years to come, the child wondered about and longed for the mother who had been taken from him.

When the baby grew into boyhood, he had a strong desire to learn. Sarah found an old children's book and taught the boy to read. Moses showed him how to do his numbers. This only whetted the child's appetite to learn more.

The school in the area only allowed white children. Oftentimes the boy sat on the school steps, straining to hear the lessons. This was not enough.

When he turned ten, the boy found out about a school for black children, located eight miles from Moses and Sarah's farm. He was too young to walk that far every day.

Finally, when he turned twelve, the youth said good-bye to Moses and Sarah and set off on his own. Eight miles away, he would go to the school for black children. A childless couple, Andrew and Mariah, happily took him in. He helped fill an empty spot in their hearts.

In spite of seventy students being crowded in a little shack, the boy still loved school; he soaked up his lessons like a sponge. While doing laundry for his keep, he kept a book propped up, studying and scrubbing. The book he cherished the most was a Bible Andrew and Mariah gave him. He kept and read it all his life.

When he learned everything he could, the boy, now in his teens, searched for a school that could teach him more.

Before he left their home, Mariah gave him advice he would never forget: to learn as much as he could and pass on what he learned to others.

He found a ride with a family taking their wagon to Fort Scott, Kansas. He quickly learned how to cook, found a job, and became the best baker around. His meager pay provided for his schooling. On he went, from home to home, from school to school—cooking and taking in laundry.

When he became a young man, he dreamed of going to college. His dream came true when he was accepted and given a scholarship to Highland College. Sadly, when the dean met the young man and saw he was black, the offer was withdrawn.

The young man was heartbroken. He aimlessly wandered the country until he came to a town called Winterset, Iowa—not far from Des Moines. There he found a job as a chef. He started going to a church in town and met Dr. and Mrs. Milholland. Mrs. Milholland directed the church choir.

The young man told the choir director he enjoyed painting and making plants grow, but he wanted to learn to sing. She gave him singing lessons in exchange for his teaching her how to paint. The kindly couple convinced him to apply at Simpson College, a Methodist school in Indianola, Iowa. There he was accepted as an art student.

Little did he know that his art teacher's father was head of the Iowa Agricultural College in Ames. It didn't take long for the art teacher to recognize a greater talent than art in the man. She convinced him to study agricultural science instead.

Even though he wanted to pursue a career in art, the man remembered the words of Mariah. He knew he must learn more and pass it on to those in need. After much study at Iowa Agricultural College, he became America's best trained black agricultural scientist in his time. The college hired him as one of their professors. Lush soil and a new greenhouse on the college campus were at his fingertips. What more could he ask?

The man's comfortable life was disrupted when a letter came from Dr. Booker T. Washington in Tuskegee, Alabama. Dr. Washington invited the man to teach needy students at his college—some of whom even came to school barefoot. The man didn't want to leave but knew he must. At Tuskegee, he could pass on what he knew to those less fortunate.

When he arrived, he found barren, sandy red and yellow soil. A useless grade of cotton was the only thing being raised. The workers looked as sick as the cotton they picked. Students met in a small blacksmith shop. Dr. Washington showed the newcomer the school's equipment: one hoe and a blind ox.

The man immediately took his new students around to all the neighbors, collecting jars, bottles, and broken dishes. These became their lab supplies. Next he helped them make the college dump into compost piles.

The young professor's practical teachings caused the number of students to mushroom. They learned to nourish the worn-out soil by growing cowpeas, better known as black-eyed peas. From their harvest, they made meat loaf, pancakes, and casseroles.

He taught them to rotate crops. Next, they would sow nuts—a plant brought over from Africa, when their families were made slaves. Folks from nearby farms followed the professor's lead. Abundant plants growing in gardens helped remind the folks of home back in Africa.

The professor taught his students additional uses for sweet potatoes besides boiling them. Folks learned how to roast and dry them. They also made them into flour, molasses, and starch for doing laundry.

The next year they planted cotton. Not the puny kind raised in the past, but strong bushes filled with big, white cotton balls. But the boll weevil moved in and destroyed their crops.

The professor suggested farming the African nuts. Before long, they were everywhere. No one knew what to do with so many. How would the farmers manage?

The teacher didn't have an answer. He felt he had let his students and the farmers down. That night he couldn't sleep. He rose at early dawn and went for a walk in the woods. There he took the matter to God, his best Friend.

The professor, George Washington Carver, went back and locked himself in his lab for twenty-four hours. With God as his guide and little to eat, Mr. Carver came up with experiments that produced a wealth of products. All were taken from the little nuts: oil, nut milk, pats of butter, gums, pectins, cosmetics, and many others.

He convinced the local businessmen to look at his discovery. They were so impressed, the crops were given a new name. They would be called peanuts! Farmers everywhere decided to form the United Peanut Association.

Professor Carver was invited to speak about his peanut discoveries all around the country. On some occasions, he was rudely turned away from meeting places because he was black—that was, until his identity was made known.

Being mistreated never ruffled Professor Carver. He kept patiently explaining his findings and made everyone he met feel at ease.

His reputation reached Congress in Washington, D.C. When he arrived and they saw he was black, Congress was ready to laugh at his ideas. Again Professor Carver good-naturedly shared his findings. Those listening soon changed their minds.

Professor Carver made many friends from all races and ranks of life. Almost everyone loved and respected him. One of his closest friends was Henry Ford.

Although he had achieved success, the now silvery-haired, unassuming professor always welcomed young and old, black or white, to come and learn by his side.

This humble, God-loving man was honored with the National Association for the Advancement of Colored Spingarn Medal, not only for his scientific contributions but for the help and understanding he gave to those around him.

A small park in Winterset, Iowa, is dedicated to George Washington Carver's memory. It is the same town where his music teacher and her husband, Dr. and Mrs. Milholland, once influenced the discouraged young man to go on to college.

George Washington Carver was a true peacemaker. Because he was willing to let the bad go in his life and focus on the good, this fine man was used by God to develop more than the use of African nuts and sweet potatoes. He fulfilled God's calling to grow peace and hope in his garden of love.

Whose Side Is God On?

"If my people, who are called by my name,
will humble themselves and pray and seek my face
and turn from their wicked ways,
then will I hear from heaven
and will forgive their sin
and will heal their land."

2 Chronicles 7:14 niv

Troubles and uncertainties of this world press in from all sides. They batter our lives' doors daily. We are constantly confronted with wars, rumors of wars, earthquakes, violence, lying, stealing, volcanoes, storms, poverty, and hunger. The list goes on.

Many times we hesitate to turn on the news because of our world's crises. When disaster strikes and our countries go into mourning, we rush to our churches in search of comfort and strength. "What if? What if?" we often say.

Whose side is God on during these troublesome times? Where can we find peace? Is God truly watching over us? How strong is our military power without our depending on God?

I believe God isn't on our side, or the sides of those we unite with. Neither is He taking the side of our enemies. God is on the side of right.

When God gave His Son Jesus to die on the cross for our sins, He didn't make the sacrifice for only one certain group of people. We are all unworthy of His love and protection. He gave His Son so whoever believes in Him will not spiritually perish but have everlasting life.

Let us take our focus off the heartache and insecurity of this world and center it on Jesus Christ. Let us pray fervently for world peace. In love, let us pray for people to know Him as their Savior—no matter if they are friends or foes.

God really does answer our prayers. Isn't it awesome that we can pray for someone we don't even know, clear across the world? Our prayers are free and unrestrained! The Bible says a righteous prayer is filled with power—a power far greater than any we as human beings can conjure up. We don't need to get reservations from God. Neither are we required to have airline tickets. Our heavenly Father is here and on the other side of the world at the same time—every minute, every hour, every day. All we need to do is open our battered doors and communicate with Him.

The next time we turn on the news or experience something wrong, let's consider grabbing a tablet and jotting down reminders about people and circumstances we can pray for. As we do so, *we* become the peacemakers. While we continue focusing on the things of God, He will keep us in perfect peace.

GRACIOUS FORGIVING

"And when you stand praying,
if you hold anything against anyone, forgive him,
so that your Father in heaven
may forgive you your sins."

MARK 11:25 NIV

We all face disagreements. The sad part is, unkind words are said and feelings get hurt. If not dealt with by serious prayer and concern for the other person's needs, hurt feelings can fester into a grudge-bearing, deadly cancer to the soul.

Conflict isn't always bad. To be productive, it requires an equal balance of honesty, love, and acceptance. Mostly, it takes a triple dose of love and forgiveness, no matter who is right.

Like riding river rapids, we may feel pretty battered in the process. But if we obey our guide, the Lord Jesus, we will make it through intact.

Often, the roughest part of conflict is being flexible so we can obey God's will. We don't *always* have to be right. We don't need to be afraid to admit when we're wrong. Sometimes knowing who is right or wrong is far less important than caring and trying to understand how the other person feels. In order to do these things, we must yield to the Lord as He carries us over the bumpy rocks. In the midst of it all, He manages to cleanse our hearts and change our stubborn wills to comply with His own. After we submit to His leading, and let our pride go, God makes our lives as sweet and pure as sparkling water.

No one comes out the winner in a conflict unless the winner is God working in our hearts. He soothes and heals and calms our anxieties. He helps us forgive, look beyond each other's faults, and care about one another with a God-filled, unconditional love. Even when we don't agree in the end, God wants us to have enough graciousness to accept the outcome.

We round the bend to the quiet waters of resolution that we have sought. We finally cross the line from conflict to peace. Our Lord and counselor restores and heals us. As we look back and see where we were wrong, we can thank God for His forgiveness, guidance, and relief in heart and mind.

The God of peace gives perfect peace to those whose hearts are stayed upon Him.

Charles Spurgeon, 1834–1892

Slice of Serenity

"'And in this place I will grant peace,' declares the Lord *Almighty."*

Haggai 2:9 niv

I watch the sun silently raise night's ebony curtain. It winks a cheerful hello through the misty veil and breaks through the clouds with resplendent glory. I set my Bible aside and push away from my laptop computer. I stretch, slip my coat on over my sweats, and step out of the ocean-side cabin our friends Ron and Susan have so graciously loaned me for a few days.

Clear, salty breezes brush against my face and revitalize my lungs. My unwilling feet begin the brisk walk I need. It's better than any cup of coffee.

"Thank You, God, for providing me peace away from my busy world," I whisper. "Thank You for my time alone with You."

I walk a short distance on a fishing dock. The rhythmic slapping waves soothe my soul. After a few minutes, I return to the cabin—to my Bible, my computer, my writing.

What dear Christians friends, Ron and Susan. How thankful I am for their being peacemakers—and for making it possible for me to escape a busy life and experience this little slice of serenity.

Come unto Me!

"Come unto Me!" It is the Saviour's voice—
The Lord of life, who bids thy heart rejoice;
O weary heart, with heavy cares opprest,
"Come unto Me, and I will give you rest."

Nathaniel Norton, late 1800s

Let Me Experience Peace

May the God of peace. . .
equip you with everything good for doing his will,
and may he work in us what is pleasing to him,
through Jesus Christ,
to whom be glory for ever and ever. Amen.

Hebrews 13:20–21 niv

Father, I get so frustrated about all the fear and confusion in this world. I wish it would go away. If I'm not careful, I pick up the negative mind-set and become of no use to You. Help my outlook. Let me experience the calm You promise.

Grant peace to this hurting world. Help those who suffer and are at war. Show them Your love. Place within their hearts a hunger for You and an assurance of Your peace that passes all understanding.

Bring to me Your goodness, so I can do Your will and help pass on Your loving-kindness and comfort to those with whom I come in contact. Make me what You want me to be. Let me glorify You in all I say and do.

Bless my family and friends, Lord, and grant them Your perfect peace. Keep me within the boundaries of Your will, I pray. Each day as I serve You, cause Your face to shine upon me and show me Your graciousness.

While walking life's road with You by my side, I thank You for showering me with Your loving mercy and providing me Your peace. In Jesus' name, amen.

Blessed Are. . .

THE PERSECUTED

"Blessed are those who are
persecuted for righteousness' sake,
For theirs is the kingdom of heaven.
Blessed are you when they revile and persecute you,
and say all kinds of evil against you
falsely for My sake."

MATTHEW 5:10–11 NKJV

Patty's Blessing

Dear friends,
do not be surprised at
the painful trial you are suffering,
as though something strange were happening to you.
But rejoice that you participate in
the sufferings of Christ,
so that you may be overjoyed
when his glory is revealed.
If you are insulted because of the name of Christ,
you are blessed,
for the Spirit of glory and of God rests on you.
If you suffer, it should not be as a
murderer or thief
or any other kind of criminal,
or even as a meddler.
However, if you suffer as a Christian,
do not be ashamed,
but praise God that you bear that name.

1 Peter 4:12–16 NIV

Hot tears welled in Patty's eyes as she walked out the door. Her coworker Beth had been criticizing her for living a Christian life. Beth's lies to their manager had caused Patty to be fired. She couldn't believe Beth would do such a thing. Why?

Patty was so angry at Beth she never wanted to see her again. How could she get past the hurt? She thought all things were supposed to work for good when a Christian loved the Lord. There was only one way through her problem: to take her bitterness and need for work to the Lord in prayer.

To her surprise, Patty found another job in just a couple of days, better than the one she had before. Through God's help she managed to let go of the hurt Beth had caused and forgive her.

Patty's new job required more responsibility, but she was up to it. She took classes to improve her skills and threw herself into her new position. Patty wanted to do her best work possible. She was thankful to God for her new job. Before long, she was promoted to assistant manager.

One day while at work, Patty glanced up in time to see Beth walk through the door. Beth was there to apply for work. Both Patty and Beth were surprised to see one another. Old anger boiled in Patty until she felt God speak to her heart.

Patty invited Beth to be seated for an interview. Beth told how she had been caught lying and was fired. She hung her head in shame, asking Patty's forgiveness for what she had done in the past.

God nudged Patty a second time to forgive Beth and give her another chance. It proved fruitful. Beth became one of Patty's best and most faithful employees.

Her greatest blessing came when she and Beth finally prayed together and Beth accepted Jesus as her Savior. Patty's experience proved that things really do work together for good when we love and obey God.

Our heavenly Father
never takes anything
from His children unless
He means to give them something better.

GEORGE MUELLER, 1805–1898

Watch out for the Bears

Don't be selfish;
don't live to make
a good impression on others.
Be humble, thinking of others
as better than yourself.
Don't just think about your own affairs,
but be interested in others, too,
and in what they are doing.
Your attitude should be the kind
that was shown us by Jesus Christ.

Philippians 2:3–5 TLB

Fluffy white clouds danced across the sky, casting blue-gray shadows on the nearby forest. Huckleberries growing between the garden and the trees glistened in occasional rays of sunshine. Cool, refreshing gusts of wind ruffled our hair, while Steven and I scampered about in play between the garden and house.

In spite of wanting to pick the huckleberries, we knew very well we shouldn't play near the woods. Wild animals lived there. Aunt Virginia and Uncle Theodore repeatedly warned we must watch out for the bears. If we didn't bother them or go near, they would leave us alone. One particular day, our well-learned lesson paid off.

Steven abruptly stopped what he was doing and silently nudged me. His eyes appeared wide as saucers.

"Look!" he whispered. Steven pointed toward the woods.

There, sauntering along at its leisure, was a *big* black bear. It paid us no mind. Instead, it contentedly munched on the wild huckleberries. We ran inside to tell Aunt Virginia. She immediately came outdoors with us, but the bear was gone. It took several years of convincing for my aunt and uncle to believe we really did see a bear.

From that day on, Steven and I were no longer tempted to go anywhere near the woods, even to pick berries.

* * *

We may often go about our days enthusiastically telling others of the Lord. Unfortunately, an irritating event may cause us to cringe and grind our teeth. It is then we occasionally allow someone's unsavory actions or words to obscure the love and understanding God wants us to give.

Perhaps we lose our patience and snap with a trite response we wish we were able to take back the moment it rolls off our tongues. Before we know it, the whole frustrating situation has a terrible way of bringing out the worst in us. We can become pushy, overbearing, and occasionally even ill-mannered, instead of really caring about the other person. This is when we can get ourselves into trouble and have a "bear" of a temper fly back in our faces.

When we witness for God with a wealth of good intentions, we must remember we are telling the good news of His love, not the gospel according to you and me and our viewpoints on how everyone should live their lives. Gospel means *good news.* It comes from the Bible.

There are many times Christians really are persecuted for righteousness' sake. There are other times, however, when our abrasive holier-than-thou attitudes cause us to become martyrs, because of our own careless words and actions and lack of concern for how the other person feels.

Let's carefully watch out for the bears. Be honest, but don't try to irritate them. Let's ask God to season our attitudes and words. Let's try understanding where others are coming from. May God help us be genuinely interested in how someone feels and what is going on in his or her life. We may not always agree with another person's lifestyle, but we can pray for God's guidance so we can say and do what He directs. He will give us insight so we can look beyond the flaws, see the needs, and shower that person with lots of arrow prayers and God's unconditional love.

Let's *live* the gospel according to Jesus. May He help us do and say what is right in His sight and hold our standards high.

May we then love others with the same love God gives to us.

The Roughneck Rooster

If God is for us, who can be against us?

Romans 8:31 NKJV

A roughneck rooster, Sasquatch, reigned over my dad's complying hens. The obnoxious, beautiful bird often strutted about, brightly colored feathers on his neck bristling, his tail royally swaying behind him. The comb on his arrogant head and the tip of his curved tail feathers often touched. The rooster had been transported to Washington from Iowa, where farmers had labeled him an exotic bird. Neurotic was more like it! Back and forth he marched, like a grandly decorated army sergeant.

The only persons who could trust the feisty creature were Dad and my daughter-in-law, Stayci. Even the man who delivered the propane oil to Dad's vacation trailer was afraid of the intimidating beast. Yet every time Dad approached Sasquatch, the rooster fluttered to his shoulder and nestled up to him like a dove. Because of his fondness for the watchdog rooster, Dad tolerated Sasquatch's misbehavior. He frequently warned those coming to his home to be on the lookout.

Our two-year-old grandson, Harrison, didn't handle Sasquatch very well. Our son and daughter-in-law lived next door to Dad at the time. Harrison appeared leery of Sasquatch. He watched him with saucer-shaped eyes every time the rooster came in sight. Sasquatch soon picked up on Harrison's fear. The rooster began chasing him whenever given the chance. Each time, Harrison frantically ran for his front porch, with Sasquatch gleefully padding behind him. The rooster's intimidating feathers rust-led, accompanied by brawny squawks and crows.

One day while Harrison was playing in the

yard, out came Sasquatch—neck feathers bristling. Little Harrison determinedly stood his ground. Sasquatch strategically raked his spiky feet in the dirt. Though trembling in his sneakers, Harrison stood tall. The little guy never said a word; he just stared that rooster right in the eye. All of a sudden the bird slowly turned and sauntered away. Harrison looked surprised at the outcome of this standoff. Sasquatch glanced back one more time. Strangely, the saucy bird was looking past Harrison.

When Harrison turned around, there was big, tall "Chicken Grandpa" (that's what the grandkids call him) standing behind his little great-grandson. Hands on hips, Dad made it clear to the rooster to let his great-grandson be!

Not long after, Sasquatch was traded to another farmer to rule over their chicken flock (and probably the farmer).

* * *

Like Harrison, we as Christians face roughneck roosters in our lives. Sometimes they are scary and intimidating. They can even cause us grief.

One thing to remember is we are not alone. Our heavenly Father is right there with us, fighting our battles when things get a little crazy. We belong to Him, and we are loved with an everlasting love. All we need to do is stick close to God, remain true, and allow Him to help us. When we are mistreated for living Christian lives, we must remember the Lord is our defense. He will remain near and show us a way of escape.

FAITHFULNESS BLESSED

"God was with him [Joseph]
and delivered him out of all his troubles,
and gave him favor and wisdom."

ACTS 7:9–10 NKJV

There is no doubt that Joseph gained more favor from his father than what his brothers received. Most certainly, God blessed the boy with strange dreams no one could understand. The beautiful coat of many colors Joseph's father made him and the youth's condescending dreams caused his brothers to become extremely jealous.

Joseph knew there was something very significant about the dreams. No matter what the future held, he was determined in his heart to be faithful to God in all his ways.

Joseph was only in his late teenage years when his brothers stripped him of his coat and tossed him into a pit with nothing to eat or drink. How frightened Joseph must have been when his brothers pulled him out and sold him as a slave for twenty pieces of silver to passing Ishmaelite merchants. Still, the boy, changing to manhood, was true to God.

The Ishmaelite merchants sold Joseph to Potiphar, a captain of Pharaoh's guard. Even though he desperately missed his family and wondered why his brothers had done such terrible things to him, Joseph didn't allow hatred and anger to burn within him. Surely God had him in Egypt for a purpose.

Joseph kept doing his best work as a servant. God was with him and blessed everything he did with success. Before long, the captain of Pharoah's guard noticed his servant being honest and responsible. Potiphar favored Joseph and made him overseer of the guard's house and belongings.

Joseph was becoming a handsome young man. When Potiphar's wife tried to get him to compromise his standards and commit adultery with her, Joseph would have no part of her scheme. Potiphar's wife grew furious. Because she was rejected by him, she stormed to her husband and convinced him Joseph had forced himself upon her.

Joseph was put in prison. There he stayed close to God and trusted Him. He continued to seek the Lord's direction with all his heart. In turn, God gave Joseph dreams and prophecies. Everything he dreamed, visualized, and explained to others was filled with deep insight and wisdom.

Joseph's God-given ability to interpret Pharaoh's dreams helped make it possible for the faithful prisoner of two years to be released. The status he once held in the courts was finally restored.

By this time, Joseph was thirty years old. He was appointed ruler over all of Egypt, second only to Pharaoh. God blessed him with a loving wife and family.

During a famine, his brothers came in search of food. It had been twenty years since Joseph had seen them. Twenty years since they had stripped him of his coat, thrown him into a pit, then mercilessly sold him to merchants. Now Joseph sat before them on the throne of Egypt. He knew them immediately, but the brothers didn't recognize the strong, handsome man. Instead of a coat of many colors, Joseph wore luxurious, royal robes. Tears of joy that were impossible to hide filled his eyes.

God gave Joseph enough compassion to love

and forgive his brothers in spite of what they had done to him. The boy-turned-ruler welcomed his father, his brothers, and their families into his new homeland in Egypt. He made sure they were well cared for.

Although terrible things happened to Joseph, God worked it all together for good, sending him to a foreign land to help numerous people, including his own family. Joseph never expected all the blessings God bestowed upon him. But God rewarded him for being faithful.

Like Joseph, we also face times when we are persecuted. When we do, let us take our focus off self-pity, anger, and bitterness. Let us instead trust and honor God in all situations. He sees the big picture and can use us to work things together for good and glorify our Father.

O Jesus, I Have Promised

O Jesus, I have promised
To serve Thee to the end;
Be Thou forever near me,
My Master and my Friend;
I shall not fear the battle
If Thou art by my side,
Nor wander from the pathway
If Thou wilt be my Guide.

O let me feel Thee near me,
The world is ever near;
I see the sights that dazzle,
The tempting sounds I hear;
My foes are ever near me,
Around me and within;
But, Jesus, draw Thou nearer,
And shield my soul from sin.

O Jesus, Thou hast promised
To all who follow Thee
That where Thou art in glory
There shall Thy servant be;
And, Jesus, I have promised
To serve Thee to the end;
O give me grace to follow
My Master and my Friend.

John E. Bode, 1816–1874

I Give It All to You

"For whoever desires to save his life will lose it, but whoever loses his life for My sake will find it."

Matthew 16:25 NKJV

I could hear them talking behind my back again today, Lord. Why do these people I work with make fun of me for being a Christian? Having this happen is a new experience for me. I'm just starting this job, and I want to do well. Please show me how to be faithful and do what's right.

Some people are required to make huge sacrifices because they love You. Others are forced to give their lives unless they reject You. Can I ever be that strong? The only way is through Your power. I give it all to You, Lord, and trust You to help me.

In a way, I feel complimented that they can tell by my life that I love You, Lord. Do they feel uncomfortable around me? Or are they simply trying to test me to see if my relationship with You is real? Perhaps they simply don't understand what it means to be a Christian.

Well, Lord, here goes. Once again, I give it all to You, on or off of my job. I'm going to focus on You and ride this thing out. I'm kind of curious what will happen next. Thank You for being with me, Lord.

* * *

Here I am, Lord. Let me tell You about my day (as if You don't already know). Today when I was at work, someone asked me if I ever had any fun. I told about how I have some great times with my family and friends, how I enjoy doing things at our church. I explained that we even have a good time on New Year's Eve at our church—how the families celebrate together, and no one drinks and has a hangover the next day.

* * *

A funny thing happened at work today, Lord. A group of coworkers was clustered together telling dirty jokes. When I walked by, one of them hushed the others and explained I didn't like to hear that kind of thing. What a compliment, Lord! I felt honored they would consider me. I just smiled and went about my work.

Help me not to be abrasive and offend. Instead, let my life be a living testimony for each one of my coworkers. If the opportunity arises, guide me in telling them about You. Please speak to each person, I pray. How I long for my friends at work to know You.

* * *

Today was a rough day, Lord. Tempers were on edge. The workload was so heavy, everyone was stressed out. The whole thing brought out the worst in me. I lost my patience, and I know others noticed. I asked those involved to forgive me. Will You please forgive me, too?

Lord, I have another request. I know You are with me each day, but would You please send one more Christian to my workplace? It's pretty tough sometimes.

* * *

Today, someone new started working near me. Guess what? Yes, I realize You already know. Her name is Jen. She's a Christian. Thank You, Lord. Thank You for helping me give it all to You. Oh, another thing. Cheryl began asking questions about what it meant to be a Christian and how it would help with all her problems. I'm so glad. I was thrilled to talk with her. And Jen was able to talk with her also. Please help Cheryl to accept You.

Thank You for letting me come to You. I love You, Lord Jesus. Amen.

Rejoice and

Be Glad

"Rejoice and be exceedingly glad."

Matthew 5:12 NKJV

Overflowing Joy

Therefore with joy you will draw water
From the wells of salvation.
And in that day you will say:
"Praise the Lord, call upon His name;
Declare His deeds among the peoples,
Make mention that His name is exalted."

Isaiah 12:3–4 NKJV

Tornadoes of trouble often surround our lives. We wonder if our joy as Christians is being consumed by storms and droughts like barren, wasted gardens. We're often tempted to become drained, bogged down, and discouraged because of all the sad and negative things happening. Without notice, our determined, positive attitudes can plummet to bitterness and despair. We may feel outnumbered and defeated. Our outlook on life can cause us to mumble: "All is lost, and the whole world is one big, bad place."

Isn't it amazing how in our depths of despair God manages to position a strong, positive Christian in our path, just when we need one most!

Do you ever wonder where these Christians find their source of strength and joy? Is what's happening in their lives the real thing? The answer reminds me of when my husband Bob and I and our strapping young boys lived for a short time on a small farm we leased in eastern Washington.

Our only source of water was a small well. We had to always be careful not to pump the well dry. When this happened, we were forced to climb down into the well's opening with a small metal pitcher of water in hand. (We always kept the water-filled pitcher close by in the pump house.) Inside the upper part of the well, we steadied ourselves against the side of one wall, carefully drizzled in some water, and primed the pump.

Cooking and doing laundry for our family caused me to use the well's water to the limit. Surprisingly, the well tapped into a strong, underground water rivulet. The more frequently I used the well, the more its production of water gradually increased.

The owner of the farm was surprised when he found out not only was I doing dishes and laundry, I was able to water our little vegetable garden. I simply needed to pace the use of the water.

It's the same thing in our lives as Christians. Everywhere we look, we see people thirsting for Christ. We want to water and nourish those around us all the time. If we're not careful, however, we can give out more than we are able to produce. All of a sudden, we are drained and our spirits run dry.

It is then we learn to pause, pick up God's Word, and pray. When we do, we prime the pump to His living water: our source of joy and strength. As His Spirit moves, we rejoice in His love and are blessed and filled once again to overflowing.

Like the little well, we become refreshed and energized in the Lord when we make it our priority to draw from His bottomless well daily. Afterward, we are able to pass on His blessings and encouragement to others.

So goes the precious flow of His abundant living water—from drought and discouragement to priming, pumping, and seeking the Lord. At long last, He causes our wells to spring up and overflow with abundant joy. Once again, we shall rejoice in His rejuvenating love and strength.

* * *

The next time you feel drained,

remember to prime your pump of prayer.

Rejoice, Ye Pure in Heart

Rejoice, ye pure in heart;
Rejoice, give thanks and sing;
Your festal banner wave on high,
The cross of Christ your King!

Bright youth and snow-crowned age,
Strong men and maidens meek,
Raise high your free, exultant song,
God's wondrous praises speak.

With voice as full and strong
As ocean's surging praise,
Send forth the hymns our fathers loved,
The psalms of ancient days.

Yes, on through life's long path,
Still chanting as ye go,
From youth to age, by night and day,
In gladness and in woe.

Edward H. Plumptre, 1821–1891

Live your life while you have it.
Life is a splendid gift.
There is nothing small about it.

Florence Nightengale, 1820–1910

I Rejoice in Your Presence

I'm glad I could have this time with You, dear Father. It's so quiet out here on my patio. The only noise I hear is the birds and cars passing on the street. I'm pleased I was able to rise early so You and I could talk—and You and I could listen. I sip on a cup of tea, but the thirst of my soul is being satisfied from the pure, sweet waters of Your Holy Spirit. How I rejoice in Your presence.

You are so dear to me, Lord, as You minister to my soul. I thank You and praise Your name for the unfailing love You shower upon me.

I open my Bible and read of Your wonderful, countless ways. In wisdom and love, You lay them out in front of me. Thank You for Your promise of hope, courage, and guidance. I appreciate that nothing I bring to You is too great or small for You to care about. I present to You my tiny morsel of faith, as I place each of my concerns into Your capable hands.

Lead me this day, I pray. Help me be ever mindful of Your guiding, strengthening presence. Keep me calm. Help me to be gracious and courteous on the freeway, at the traffic lights, in my workplace, and especially with my loved ones at home.

When troubles belabor me, I will still rejoice in You. For You are the victor and shall guide me in handling each one. How I praise You that there are no mountainous temptations or problems uncommon to humankind. You know full well each one. Thank You for Your assurance that You will always make a way of escape or help me tunnel through my troubles. How I rejoice in Your mighty power over adversity!

When everything goes smoothly, I feel like clicking my heels. In those times, I thank You. Let me exercise caution and be mindful of Your leading. For You, above all, are my counselor and Friend.

With all my heart, I praise You, dear Lord. Through my words and actions I long to reflect Your wondrous ways so others may get to know You. In each circumstance, I will give gratitude and exult in Your holy name.

Thank You for Your righteousness. From the

beginning to the end of my day, I lift my heart to You in quiet songs of praise. In You I delight. In You I place my trust. In Your presence I rejoice.

Great Is

YOUR REWARD

"For great is your reward in heaven,
for so they persecuted the prophets
who were before you."

MATTHEW 5:12 NKJV

A Glimpse of the Savior

"Look," he said, "I see heaven open and the Son of Man standing at the right hand of God."

Acts 7:56 NIV

The anointing of God's Holy Spirit swept over Stephen whenever he shared the love of Jesus Christ with everyone who would listen. Stephen was able to do tremendous wonders through faith and power given from God.

When he stood trial before the synagogue council, Stephen probably had a tremendous desire to speak out for the Lord. No matter what would happen, he refused to back down in his belief in his Savior.

Tempers rose. Lies spewed from angry mouths. Stephen's main focus was on the Lord, rather than what would happen to him. In the midst of turmoil, the Holy Spirit completely filled him. Did Stephen's eyes fill with tears of joy when he described heaven opening and seeing the awesome glory of God?

Stephen shouted, looking heavenward, "Behold, I see the heavens opened, and the Son of man standing on the right hand of God" (Acts 7:56 KJV).

During this moment of explosive triumph, perhaps Jesus looked down at Stephen with love and compassion. Nothing else must have mattered, in light of God's indescribable power and glory.

The angry mob ran at Stephen and cast him out of the city. There they ruthlessly stoned this humble servant of the Lord.

Though surrounded by hatred and pain, God gave Stephen a glimpse of His Son, the Lord Jesus, in heaven. God's power enabled His servant to love with a holy love, as he again cried out to God: "Lord Jesus, receive my spirit" (Acts 7:59 KJV).

Could Stephen hear angels sing above the angry shouts? Did the presence of his Lord help numb the pain from hurling stones?

Stephen dropped to his knees and prayed for his besiegers: "Lord, lay not this sin to their charge" (Acts 7:60 KJV).

According to the Bible, he then simply went to sleep. No longer was he the victim of anger and brutality. Stephen's glimpse of the Lord Jesus had come into full view. At last, he arrived home in heaven with the Lord. There, Stephen surely received his reward.

Yet good came from the cruelty. During the stoning, witnesses laid their clothes at the feet of a young man called Saul. Saul never forgot that scene of Stephen's encounter with the Savior. Later, Saul had an encounter of his own with Jesus.

The love Stephen showed during his final moments here on earth was the first step by Saul (later named Paul) in answering the Savior's invitation to become a soul winner for God.

REWARD FOR A BROKEN HEART

"Your old men will dream dreams, your young men will see visions."

JOEL 2:28 NIV

He was born in Fort Dodge, Iowa, in 1914 as the youngest of seven children. His family moved from there to Greeley, Colorado, then on to Los Angeles, California. When he was near twelve years of age, his parents joined the Grace Church of the Nazarene, and the boy accepted the Lord as his Savior.

By the time he became a teenager, he began serving God as a preacher on downtown street corners. In spite of not considering himself very talented while attending school at Pasadena Nazarene College, the young adult became student body president. He had quite a sense of humor and enjoyed pulling pranks on his friends.

At the end of his junior year, he married a Nazarene minister's daughter. Three children blessed their marriage.

During the next several years, he followed God's call to serve as a traveling evangelist in the West Coast Church of the Nazarene, an evangelist for World Christian Fundamentals Association, a manager of Eureka Jubilee Singers, a Christian filmmaker, and an assistant minister to his father-in-law in Los Angeles Evangelistic Center. Later, he was ordained by the First Baptist Church of Wilmington, California.

He dedicated himself to working with young people in Youth for Christ. There he led a YFC rally in Seattle, Washington. Soon after, he became Youth for Christ vice president at large.

One day Madame Chiang Kai-shek asked the man to bring Youth for Christ to China for a series of rallies. During the rallies in China, approximately eighteen thousand people came to the Lord. The disabled, poor, outcast, and orphaned in China broke the man's heart. He had no doubt what God was calling him to do. He had to help these people and others like them.

From then on, Robert Willard Pierce displayed an overwhelming drive to put every ounce of energy he had into raising money to help needy children from China. Because of the Chinese Communist

Revolution, he had to leave China. He went on to help others in South Korea. Through his labors, World Vision organization was born.

Bob Pierce formed a Korean Orphan Choir. The choir traveled all over, helping to raise money for the orphaned. Bob spoke wherever people throughout the world would listen, asking them to give financial help for impoverished children. His ministry of mercy expanded from Korea to Taiwan, then into other countries.

His heartfelt and memorable statement still rings through history:

"Let my heart be broken with the things that break the heart of God."

World Vision expanded into a huge mission organization. Known as Dr. Bob Pierce, the missionary's dream to help poor children across the world was coming true. Sadly, the pain and poverty he had witnessed caused him to become engulfed in his work to the point where nothing else mattered nearly as much. Because of this, he neglected his own health. He died of leukemia.

Others picked up Dr. Pierce's torch of service. World Vision has now grown to reach people all over the world. What began with Dr. Pierce's simple love for the children and heeding God's call far exceeded the dedicated missionary's greatest dreams of what God would accomplish in years to come. Surely Dr. Bob Pierce's greatest reward is in heaven.

May God richly bless World Vision workers and givers as they continue to reach out and help the disabled, the outcast, the poor, and the lost in our needy world.

"God's gifts put man's best dreams to shame."

ELIZABETH BARRETT BROWNING, 1806–1861

THE GREATEST REWARD EVER

And the ransomed of the LORD shall return,
And come to Zion with singing,
With everlasting joy on their heads.
They shall obtain joy and gladness,
And sorrow and sighing shall flee away.

ISAIAH 35:10 NKJV

What is the greatest reward we can possibly receive in heaven? Will it be the absence of sickness, pain, sorrow, sin? Will it be complete, uninhibited joy?

Will the ultimate reward go to those who gave their lives for their Savior? What about the great leaders, missionaries, and evangelists who gave their all? Or faithful Christians who taught church schools, trained others, or raised their own children to love and serve God? Will there be a reward for the ones who accepted Christ in the ebb of their earthly lives?

To me the greatest reward is to be able to see our Savior face-to-face. There we will finally be in His holy presence and experience His joy for all eternity.

I Want to Be with You

"And God will wipe away every tear from their eyes."

Revelation 7:17 NIV

What will it be like when I finally get to be with You in heaven, Lord? Will there be more Christians than anyone can count? Will they come from every nationality, rank, and race? What about my loved ones? I look forward with longing to being reunited with them.

Will everyone be dressed in robes of white like it says in the Bible, singing praises to You, our God and King? I wonder, Lord, if I'll finally be able to see the angels gathered around Your throne.

I want to be with You, dear Lord. I look forward to joining in the praise and saying: "Amen: Blessing, and glory, and wisdom, and thanksgiving, and honour, and power, and might, be unto our God for ever and ever. Amen" (Revelation 7:12 KJV).

How unworthy I feel to enter Your glorious kingdom. It is only because You shed Your blood for me, washed my sins away, and made me white as snow that I can hope to attain such joy.

I yearn for when there will be no more hunger or thirst—no more sin, sickness, or pain. No longer will I feel any sadness, for You have promised to wipe away every one of my tears. All the struggles and heartache I have experienced on this earth will have been worth it. They will pale in Your radiant glory!

I can't even consider any reward I will receive in heaven. Whatever good I have done is counted as nothing in comparison with Your grace.

I want to kneel before Your throne, ask for Your forgiveness once more, and tell You how much I love You. Because of Your forgiving love, You have promised to remember my repented sins no more. My greatest reward will be for You to step forward and reach out Your hand. Perhaps You will look at me, then simply help me to my feet. I long for You to wrap me in Your arms and say, "Well done, my good and faithful servant. Welcome home."

A Crown of Rejoicing

O crown of rejoicing that's waiting for me,
When finished my course, and when Jesus I see,
And when from my Lord comes the sweet
sounding word:
"Receive, faithful servant, the joy of thy Lord."

O wonderful song that in glory I'll sing,
To Him who redeem'd me, to Jesus my King;
All glory and honor to Him shall be given,
And praises unceasing forever in heaven.

O joy everlasting when heaven is won,
Forever in glory to shine as the sun:
No sorrow nor sighing—these all fly away;
No night there, no shadows—'tis one endless day.

O wonderful name which the glorified hear,
The "new name" which Jesus bestows on us there;
To join him that o'ercometh 'twill only be given,
Blest sign of approval, our welcome to heaven.

Rev. J. B. Atchinson, late 1800s

The Salt

OF THE EARTH

"You are the salt of the earth;
but if the salt loses its flavor,
how shall it be seasoned?"

MATTHEW 5:13 NKJV

A Bridge for the Future

Do your best to present yourself
to God as one approved,
a workman who does not need to be ashamed
and who correctly handles the word of truth.

2 Timothy 2:15 niv

There's an area just outside Miles City, Montana, that I love to visit every time I have the chance. It was where my dad grew up: It's called Mizpah.

Dad and his three brothers spent most of their youthful years on the old homeplace. The boys were kept too busy to get into trouble by helping their ma and pa tend a 320-acre farm.

I wish I could have known Grandpa. He died before my time. Grandma and I were close. Her love for the Lord made a permanent impact on my life. She lived into her early eighties.

From what Dad tells me, his mother and dad were constantly helping other people. Their door was always open to friends and strangers. Everyone liked to gather at their house. Grandpa and Grandma were the kind of folks who wanted to make a better way for the younger ones' future.

A couple of miles before you reach the old homeplace stands the Powder River Bridge. The old well-built bridge has become a landmark. Some have wanted to tear it down. The bridge, however, is still in good shape. Those who care about their heritage have managed to influence Custer County authorities to keep and maintain it.

In 1923, a terrible flash flood came. A wall of water from Powder River crashed into the original bridge and wiped it out.

Folks had to manage for a long time by crossing the river on horseback. That was also the only way they could move cattle to the other side of the river. Powder River was—and still is—treacherous. It contains deadly, unpredictable currents and quicksand. The river shifts constantly.

A neighbor down the road was the only man strong enough to row a boat and transport people back and forth across the river. Everyone knew something had to be done to make it easier for those attempting to cross the river in years to come.

Finally, Custer County was able to hire a contractor to build a new bridge. Workers throughout the area were hired on as hands to help build it. My uncle Bill, being the eldest son, was one of them.

Handsaws scraped and hammers pounded while the men quickly built a kitchen, eating area, and bunkhouse.

All the construction on the bridge had to be done by hand. Some of the men climbed clear to the top of the bridge to work. Others below heated rivets in a small blast furnace, took them out with tongs, and tossed them to the men on top of the bridge. The workers overhead caught the white-hot rivets in a funnel and secured them immediately into place. It was a dangerous, exhausting job, but one everyone did with pride.

Upon its completion in 1926, the bridge stood tall and proud. Folks from miles around came out for the dedication. Even the news reporters were there. I still have a copy of the newspaper picture with Uncle Bill, Dad, Uncle Russell, the rest of their family, and many others standing by their grand accomplishment. A job well-done. A gift for future generations.

Although a disastrous flood caused a lot of inconvenience and work, much good came from it. A fine bunch of people had united to make an even better bridge for the future.

* * *

Like the Powder River Bridge, we, too, experience disasters in our lives. Hopefully, we learn from them. Through each one, may we unite and work feverishly to build a better future, physically, mentally, and spiritually for those following us.

May God bless our descendants with what we have learned, along with their newly found wisdom and nurturing from the Lord. May they, too, build better bridges for the future. May each endeavor be filled with love, joy, patience, and peace.

* * *

" 'Tis easy enough to be pleasant,
when life flows like a song.
But the man worthwhile is the one who
will smile when everything goes dead wrong."

ELLA WHEELER WILCOX
NOVEMBER 5, 1850–OCTOBER 30, 1919

The Bridge-Builder

An old man, going down a lone highway
Came at the evening, cold and gray,
To a chasm vast and wide and steep,
With waters rolling cold and deep.
The old man crossed in the twilight dim;
The sullen stream had no fears for him.
But he turned when safe on the other side,
And built a bridge to span the tide.

"Old man," said a fellow pilgrim near,
"You are wasting your strength with building here.
Your journey will end with the ending day,
You never again will pass this way.
You've crossed the chasm, deep and wide,
Why build you this bridge at eventide?"

The builder lifted his old gray head.
"Good friend, in the path I have come," he said,
"There followed after me today
A youth whose feet must pass this way.
The chasm that was naught to me
To that fair-haired youth may a pitfall be;
He, too, must cross in the twilight dim—
Good friend, I am building this bridge for him."

Will Allen Dromgoole, 1860–1934

LEGACY OF WISDOM

Who is wise and understanding among you?
Let him show it by his good life,
by deeds done in the humility
that comes from wisdom.

JAMES 3:13 NIV

Aunt Virginia and Uncle Theodore's sturdy farmhouse seemed to belong nestled near a legendary maple tree in the yard. The old house wasn't elaborate. It offered a country-type porch. No pillars. It was just a place where everyone was made to feel welcome.

If you were to step onto the porch, you would find a pantry at one end and the farmhouse back door. Everyone entered Aunt Virginia and Uncle Theodore's home through the back entrance. Inside the door was the kitchen, big enough for all of us kids. It radiated warmth and love.

My favorite time of day was breakfast. As we lumbered downstairs, our noses followed the tantalizing aromas wafting from the kitchen. While Aunt Virginia and the older girls cooked on the woodstove, my teenage cousin Neil tossed my smaller cousin Steven and me in the air and made us laugh. Everyone patiently listened to Steven and me proudly count to one hundred, again and again.

We all gathered around the table and chattered away while contentedly slurping hot chocolate and filling up on eggs and pancakes covered with home-churned butter and molasses.

Aunt Virginia was a good cook. Everything she made was flavored just right. Not only did she properly season food for our stomachs, she also amply and tastefully supplied our spiritual food. Many morsels of wisdom were passed my way, always given with just the right amount of seasoning. Aunt Virginia seemed to know what to say or do at the perfect time, and when to say nothing at all.

The old farmhouse is gone now. The lessons learned there from Aunt Virginia are preserved and will remain with me forever.

May God grant us the right amount of sweetness, a few granules of the salt of His Holy Spirit, and proper timing, so He can use us to bless others.

* * *

Write upon your heart to seize the opportunities
God gives you every day.
Be a blessing for Him,
with rightly seasoned words, filled with wisdom.

Look and Live

I've a message from the Lord, Hallelujah!
The message unto you I'll give;
'Tis recorded in His Word, Hallelujah!
It is only that you "look and live."

I've message full of love, Hallelujah!
A message, oh my friend, for you;
'Tis a message from above, Hallelujah!
Jesus said it, and I know 'tis true.

Life is offered unto you, Hallelujah!
Eternal life thy soul shall have,
If you'll only look to Him, Hallelujah!
Look to Jesus, who alone can save.

I will tell you how I came, Hallelujah!
To Jesus when He made me whole:
'Twas believing on His name, Hallelujah!
I trusted, and He saved my soul.

"Look and live," my brother, live,
Look to Jesus now and live;
'Tis recorded in His Word, Hallelujah!
It is only that you "look and live."

W. A. Ogden, 1841–1897

Season My Words

Let your conversation be always
full of grace,
seasoned with salt,
so that you may know
how to answer everyone.

Colossians 4:6 niv

Not long ago You gave me the chance to tell someone about You, Lord. I found myself shaking in my shoes—and didn't do anything. I'm sorry. It wasn't that I'm ashamed of You. I was simply afraid of saying the wrong things. I wondered if she'd laugh at me. Worse yet, what if she grew angry?

I really care about people, Lord. Unfortunately, I have a tendency to be a "fixer." That's when I get myself into trouble and stick my foot in my mouth. I know You remind me over and over that I'm here to show love. *You're* the One who is here to fix things.

Lord, I ask You to help me overcome my fear of telling others about You. Teach me how to be watchful of what I say. Somehow open the door to my friend's heart so I can reveal the remarkable way You can become her personal Savior.

Guide me in what I say so my words are always filled with graciousness. Season my words. Let them not be savorless and watered-down. In my zeal to share, neither let my words be too salty, lest I drive her away.

I know she's going through some hard times. She seems like a little dried-up spring. Parched. Lacking joy. Her life is entangled in so many problems. I long for her to get to know You and not be a slave to sin and sadness. Please help her so she can experience the true, bountiful joy from Your unlimited springs of living water. Teach her how to turn everything in her life over to You.

I don't have all the answers to her problems, Lord, but You do. Grant me the wisdom to listen to her and care about how she feels. Remind me how Your Holy Spirit has the ability to meet her needs and guide her.

I'm excited about what You do in my life, Lord. Perhaps all I need to do is tell her how You have changed my life and still help me each day. When I read in Your Bible, it tells me about the Gospels Matthew, Mark, Luke, and John. I've learned that "gospel" means "good news." Good news, I certainly have. Please make an opening,

Lord, when You want me to tell about You. Then help me be brave enough to follow Your lead.

Well, here she comes, Lord. I'm tuning in to You for guidance and help.

* * *

Hmmm. That wasn't so bad, Lord. In fact, it was downright exciting to see how Your Holy Spirit worked through my words and spoke to her heart. Thank You for being here.

The next time You urge me to tell Your good news, season my words again. I'll give You all the praise. In Jesus' name, amen.

Let Your

Light Shine

"You are the light of the world.
A city that is set on a hill cannot be hidden.
Nor do they light a lamp
and put it under a basket,
but on a lampstand,
and it gives light to all who are in the house.
Let your light so shine before men,
that they may see your good works
and glorify your Father in heaven."

Matthew 5:14–16 NKJV

GRANDMA'S LAMP

The path of the righteous is like
the first gleam of dawn,
shining ever brighter
till the full light of day.

PROVERBS 4:18 NIV

Do everything without complaining or arguing,
so that you may become blameless and pure,
children of God without fault in a crooked
and depraved generation,
in which you shine
like stars in the universe.

PHILIPPIANS 2:14–15 NIV

Weather back in Mizpah, Montana, during the winter is so cold sometimes it isn't fit for man or beast. That was the case during a brutal winter in 1937.

Dad was only eighteen. Although the weather was bad, his brother Bill still carried on his job doing roadwork about four or five miles from their home. Dad was planning to ride his horse, Coon, out to check on Bill, then return home.

Dad knew he wouldn't make it home before dark. Everything grew pitch-black when night fell. There were no streetlights. Country folks didn't have electricity back then. Neighbors lived miles apart.

To make things worse, snow began flying and drifting like crazy. Dad's mother was concerned about him getting lost in the storm. She told him she would place a kerosene lamp in the window for him. The homeplace sat at the end of their mile-long private road. A lamp could be plainly seen from a long distance.

Dad reached Bill, saw he was all right, and dropped off some food. Dark, lowering clouds made nightfall come fast. Things couldn't have been blacker. No moon. No stars. Snow flurries worsened and drifted so high, not a fence post could be found. The usual emerald trees crowned with snow didn't break the darkness.

In spite of the elements, Dad wasn't worried. His horse, Coon, was one of the best. Coon bent his head low while Dad hunched over his back. Icy winds whistled hollow, mournful songs and tore at Coon and at Dad's clothing as they pressed toward home.

Dad recalls how bad it was: "It was dark all right, when I was headin' home. Pitch-black, it was. Just inky black sky, 'n cuttin' wind, 'n white snow everywhere."

After riding a few miles, Dad finally spotted a shaft of light from the lamp his mother had placed in the window. Nothing to worry about. Dad confidently kept riding in the direction of the light. He looked forward to getting home, safe and warm.

But something was wrong. The light moved! Wasn't it the lamp? He wondered if the light came from a passing car, traveling on the other side of the river.

It was plain to Dad that he had lost his bearings. Getting turned around was way too dangerous in such weather, especially at night. He studied the situation. Who had the most sense at this point? He? Or the horse? It didn't take long for Dad to decide.

He dropped the reins, let them rest on the saddle horn, and gave Coon his head. Dad knew his horse could bring them safely home.

Coon did just that. Before long, rider and horse worked their way down the mile-long road to the house.

After he got the horse settled in the barn and went inside the house, Dad found out what had been wrong. While he was watching the lamp, his mother moved it from one window to another to make it more visible.

* * *

Think for a moment of our spiritual lights being like Grandma's lamp. We may already be letting our lights shine for those around us, the way God wants us to do. But we must be careful to remain consistent and dependable in our walk with the Lord. Others are watching and counting on us to lead the way. Let's set a straight course as we walk our spiritual walk, so they can see a good example. In this way, the light we are shining will lead them straight to the heavenly Father.

Let There Be Light

Light is shed upon the righteous
and joy on the upright in heart.
Rejoice in the Lord, you who are righteous,
and praise his holy name.

Psalm 97:11–12 NIV

When night fell on the farm at Aunt Virginia and Uncle Theodore's, someone skillfully lit a kerosene lamp. The small flame soon illuminated the lamp's chimney, broke through the evening darkness, and radiated warmth and love throughout the room.

We didn't have electricity on the farm. We obviously didn't have television, either. Instead, we found ways to entertain ourselves. Sometimes we hung a sheet between the living and dining room and placed the lamp on the dining room table. All of us younger kids gathered in the dark living room and cheered our older siblings on while they dramatically entertained us with one great shadow performance after another.

Minnie and Happy's family lived down the road a way. They also had a special way of providing fun for friends and family. Minnie and Happy had a generator. On Friday nights after the sun went down, Happy fired up the generator. The fragrance of popcorn and of homemade fudge cooking on the woodstove filled the house. We gathered in the living and dining room and sat in the dark. Minnie turned on the big old radio. We listened and laughed together at the funny stories on "My Friend Erma" and munched popcorn and fudge to our hearts' content.

Some of Aunt Virginia's neighbors weren't quite as nice to be around. Still, my aunt and uncle treated them kindly. They continually let their lights of God's love shine to those around them.

Aunt Virginia always made sure we had plenty of ice in the icebox. The pantry window was opened at night to let the cool air in. That way, the fresh milk from their cow would keep. By morning, rich, yellow cream had risen. One of our jobs as kids was to churn the butter. Some of the cream would be held back for special treats. Often, different ones would take turns rapidly cranking the old mixer and making whipped cream. Afterward, Aunt Virginia prepared her famous mouthwatering cream puffs.

On cold nights, we trooped up to bed and nestled between flannel sheets. My older cousin Bev had carefully placed jars, filled with hot water from the stove and wrapped in towels, at the foot of the bed to keep our feet warm. She and I often crawled into bed and curled up like spoons. One of us traced pictures on the other's back, and we took turns guessing what was drawn until we drifted off to sleep.

Security. Love, provided by word and deed, and an ample amount of wisdom. Light from hearing God's Word. Prayer. The presence of His Holy Spirit. It was and still is all-encompassing and everlasting.

* * *

God created a phenomenal light even before He made the earth. The sun and moon and stars burst forth and pierced the endless darkness, reflecting His magnificent glory. It was the beginning of countless powerful things to come.

When the Israelites left Egypt in search of the Promised Land, God led them with a pillar of cloud by day and a pillar of fire at night. When God's tabernacle was made, lamps filled with oil were carefully placed inside to change darkness to light.

Job recalled the light God had shed upon him before he was forced to suffer. Job never lost hope that God's light would once again shine on him. Through all his heartache, this man remained faithful. God in turn blessed Job abundantly.

David prayed for the light of God's face to shine upon him and his people. He recognized God was truly the light of his salvation and his source of joy.

Jesus taught how He was and is the Light of the World. He explained that He wants us to reflect His wonderful light and hope to those around us.

As long as we follow His righteous and holy ways, we won't walk in darkness. Instead, our entire beings will be full of light, with the Holy Spirit illuminating our way. If we begin to stray, His light helps pull us back to the right path. He paves the way so we can keep from stumbling. And if we should fall, He is always there to help us up, so we can start over again.

The apostle John tells us:

God is light; in him there is no darkness at all. If we claim to have fellowship with him yet walk in the darkness, we lie and do not live by the truth. But if we walk in the light, as he is in the light, we have fellowship with one another, and the blood of Jesus, his Son, purifies us from all sin.

If we claim to be without sin, we deceive ourselves and the truth is not in us. If we confess our sins, he is faithful and just and will forgive us our sins and purify us from all unrighteousness. 1 JOHN 1:5–9 NIV

Don't lose heart. Jesus is here to light our way every single day. When hopelessness, sadness, and depression threaten to engulf us in heavy darkness, all we need to do is turn to Jesus and take His hand. He has a remarkable way of leading us through discouragement, fear, and uncertainty. When we have those days when everything seems to go wrong, we can fall asleep with a prayer on our lips and awaken to the promises of a new day. We can know full well, God is always in control. He is the Way, the Truth, the Life, and the Light.

Someday we will be in heaven. There will be no darkness. No longer will we be tempted to walk in the shadows of sin. Instead, we will be forever enveloped in His pure, brilliant light.

I can imagine it being more wonderful than

any camp meeting we have ever experienced. And, oh, the fellowship we'll enjoy with our loved ones and Christian friends! It will be a time when we can remain in the mountaintop experiences with God and not have to return to the "reality" struggles of this world.

Candles of Encouragement

We have different gifts [from God],
according to the grace given us. . . .
If it is encouraging,
let him encourage.

Romans 12:6, 8 niv

It is near the end of the school year as I write this. There are less than two weeks left. As some of you know, there are many things to be done in teaching before sending the children off for the summer. Although I love working with my students, exhaustion has set in. How I long to have more time to write.

If I'm not careful during these tiring times, I

become bogged down and discouraged. This is when I take my concerns and needs to God more than ever. After I do this, I never cease to be amazed at how He works.

I found myself at this point only a few days ago. I placed my need for strength and encouragement before God. Sure enough, He used wonderful Christian people to encourage and pray for me.

One source of strength came from a letter written by a lady from New Zealand. How she blessed my soul as she told me about her becoming a Christian and the wonderful things God was doing in her life. Not only did it warm my heart; it reminded me of what He was accomplishing throughout the world. The same Holy Spirit who ministers to me is helping people from the East to West.

The other light of encouragement passed my way was a note from my father-in-law. I had recently sent him and Mom copies of the advertisements for my books and asked them to pray for me to have strength, encouragement, and wisdom as I wrote.

This is the letter Dad and Mom sent back:

"Dear Neat,

Your letter of information about the books arrived a few days ago. We want to say how proud we are of you. As you look back over the years of hard work, long hours, sweat, and, no doubt, tears, you must feel blessed in the journey God has set you on. A job well done.

Through the times while some doubted and ignored your calling, you continued to hang in there. With the great help from the Lord Himself, your efforts were blessed and are being used by Him.

We are proud of you, Neat. Now get to work and get the next one out.

As always, we love you,
Dad and Mother Donihue"

This day is all that is good and fair.
It is too dear, with its hopes and invitations,
to waste a moment on yesterdays.

Ralph Waldo Emerson, 1803–1882

Send the Light

There's a call comes ringing o'er the restless wave,
"Send the light! Send the light!"
There are souls to rescue; there are souls to save,
Send the light! Send the light!

Let us pray that grace may everywhere abound;
Send the light! Send the light!
And a Christlike spirit everywhere be found,
Send the light! Send the light!

Let us not grow weary in the work of love,
Send the light! Send the light!
Let us gather jewels for a crown above,
Send the light! Send the light!

Send the light, the blessed gospel light;
Let it shine from shore to shore!
Send the light, the blessed gospel light;
Let it shine forevermore.

Charles H. Gabriel, 1856–1932

Flipping on the Switch

Then your light will break forth like the dawn,
and your healing will quickly appear;
then your righteousness will go before you,
and the glory of the Lord will be your rear guard.

Isaiah 58:8 niv

Father, I am constantly amazed at how You work. Here I am, going full-steam ahead with my busy schedule and all my responsibilities. Then this happens.

I glance up from my mountain of paperwork and notice one of my coworkers standing nearby. He's just looking at me and nervously shuffling from one foot to the other. I recall the cruel things he has often said about me behind my back. I cringe and want to glare at him and hint that I'm busy and don't have time to talk.

Somehow You manage to penetrate the hurt and anger within me and help me see his needs. I'm sending up a quick prayer right now, Father. As You always remind me, I'm flicking on the switch and tuning in to Your Holy Spirit. Thank You for urging me to offer him a cold soda and a chair. Thank

You for lighting my way and directing me to set my mixed feelings aside, to shove away my mountain of work, and simply listen to him.

Although I have been praying for him for a long time, I'm so surprised he has come to me. Forgive me, I pray, for when I have reacted badly. No matter if he doesn't say he is sorry or if he still goes away and talks ill of me, help me be gracious and loving enough to forgive—again and again.

Let Your light shine through me. Let my coworker see You and want to ask You to be his Savior. Help me not to get in the way of Your speaking to his heart. In Jesus' name, amen.

KEEP THE HOME FIRES BURNING

Blessed are all who fear the LORD,
who walk in his ways.
You will eat the fruit of your labor;
blessings and prosperity will be yours.
Your wife [or husband] will be like a fruitful vine
within your house;
your sons will be like olive shoots
around your table.

PSALM 128:1–3 NIV

Father, I have been rushing all week. It seems like everything I'm doing is for a worthy cause. Because I'm getting into overload and not having enough time with the ones I love the most, I cancelled a meeting I was to attend tonight. Instead, my husband, family, and I are going to have an evening together. Perhaps we'll even go out for a bite to eat, head to a park, and get away from the constantly demanding phone.

I want to serve You by helping others, but I know the ones who are to come first in my life. The meeting, along with many more, can manage without me.

Thank You for my family. How dear they are to me. I look at my loving husband and my "olive shoots," big and small, and praise You for these priceless blessings. Help me never to take them for granted. Time passes too quickly.

Remind me of my priorities, Father. Help me remember my foremost mission is at home. Teach me first to keep the home fires burning. Guide and help me each day to be a beacon of light to the ones I love the most.

If I get too carried away with added responsibilities (no matter how good they may appear), draw me back, so I put the ones I love first.

Place a spiritual hedge of thorns around them, Lord. Protect them from evil and harm. Let everything I say and do be a beacon of light to them, reflecting Your purity and love.

Consider

THE LILIES

"Consider the lilies of the field,
how they grow:
they neither toil nor spin;
and yet I say to you that even Solomon
in all his glory was not arrayed like one of these. . . .
But seek first the kingdom of God
and His righteousness,
and all these things shall be added to you.
Therefore do not worry about tomorrow,
for tomorrow will worry about its own things.
Sufficient for the day is its own trouble."

MATTHEW 6:28–29, 33–34 NKJV

In Spite of the Muck

Having said this, he [Jesus] spit on the ground,
made some mud with the saliva,
and put it on the man's eyes.
"Go," he told him, "wash in the Pool of Siloam"
(this word means Sent).
So the man went and washed, and came home seeing.

John 9:6–7 NIV

Have you ever told yourself during trying times to cheer up, things could be worse; then discovered that sure enough, they did get worse?

We often bolster our courage and trust God only to find things grow more discouraging than ever. We then fall on our knees amongst the mucky confusion and uncertainties and plead once again for God's help.

We take a deep breath, stubbornly grit our teeth, and yield once more to His plan for us. Then in His perfect way, God gently leads us. Each time we trust Him with the good and bad parts of our lives, we experience glorious victories and thank Him for bringing us through.

Had the man mentioned in the Bible, who had been blind since birth, been hoping and praying the

Savior would stop and heal him? Jesus could take away his infirmity and make everything right.

How did the man feel when Jesus came up to him? Frightened? Confused? Excited? What if he hadn't allowed the Savior to put what the blind man later learned was saliva-filled mud on his eyes? If he had known, would he have consented to such a degrading thing?

After Jesus covered the blind man's eyes with mud, the man was certainly eager to wash the muck from his eyes in the Pool of Siloam.

He must have been overwhelmed to have the ability to see for the first time and ecstatic that he obeyed Jesus. Was he afraid now to tell others this great thing Jesus had done for him? Perhaps his faith was being put to the test.

In spite of all the controversy over Jesus healing people, the man couldn't wait to tell everyone about his miraculous healing. "The man they call Jesus put mud on my eyes. I washed, and now I can see. He is a prophet!" (Paraphrased from John 9 NIV.)

When the Pharisees hurled insults at the man, he refused to back down. He would not deny the miracle Jesus had given him.

What a letdown, to be mistreated by presumably holy men of God after receiving such a marvelous blessing. Why would God be good enough to heal him, then allow him to go through all this? He soon received an answer, when Jesus came to him again:

"Do you believe in the Son of Man?" Jesus asked.

The healed man asked, "Who is he?"

"You have now seen him; in fact, he is the one speaking with you," replied the Savior.

The man surely dropped to his knees in reverent worship and replied, "Lord, I believe." Perhaps he even became one of Jesus' followers.

The next time you face frustration or disaster in your service for the Lord, keep in mind what Jesus said about the lilies of the field. Recall how He made mud from simple dirt and His spit, placed the mucky globs on the blind man's eyes, and gave him sight.

Hand over to God the muck in your life. Fear not the ups and downs. Don't give up. Allow Him to touch and lead you. Be willing to trust in Him as He answers your prayers in *His* way. Watch how He supplies your needs. He really can do it, when you totally yield all to Him, no matter the discomforts you face.

Tell everyone who will listen about the surprising things God does for you, and remember to thank Him for the help and the muck!

It may get worse for a while. But God has a way of taking the mucky bad times, working them together in His hands, and achieving far greater things than we can ever imagine.

We must take our troubles to the Lord,
but we must do more than that;
we must leave them there.

Hannah Whitall Smith, 1832–1911

Blessings of Sunshine

"I will send down showers in season;
there will be showers of blessing.
The trees of the field will yield their fruit
and the ground will yield its crops;
the people will be secure in their land.
They will know that I am the Lord."

Ezekiel 34:26–27 niv

It was late summer. Aunt Virginia, Uncle Theodore, and their neighbors were harvesting their hay. Every weather forecaster in the area was predicting several days of rain, starting in two days. Time was of great importance to get the fields harvested and the hay under cover.

The following day was the Sabbath, a day that belonged to the Lord. Rain was due to begin the morning after. I remember going to church and hearing the saints call on the Lord to hold off the rain for one more day, as they honored Him. It seems like yesterday.

Even we children joined in sincere prayer, asking God to meet our needs. If it rained before the harvest, all the crops would be ruined. What a big step of faith this was to honor the day of worship and rest.

In spite of the weather forecast, everyone held steady in prayer. Spirits fell from reading bad predictions of weather but rose from good predictions of God's assurance in His Word to care for us. God had promised in His Bible to send His rains in due season. We trusted Him to cause that season to come one day late. Amazingly, no rain fell that day.

The following day, farm engines cranked at the crack of dawn. Everyone was ready to cut and bale the ripe, white-headed hay. The sun flamboyantly pushed its yellow head above the red-orange horizon. Those old enough worked with little pause from morning until night, harvesting the hay. Scorching winds blew. Workers covered with glistening beads of sweat pushed and pulled, hauled and stacked the golden bales. As families finished, they helped the others. By the time the sun's blistering rays faded and sank behind clusters of clouds rolling steadily into the western sky, everyone's harvest was baled and safely under cover.

The next morning, rain began to pour. How thankful we were for God giving blessings of sunshine and honoring our faith in Him.

I was only about five years old, but the lesson I learned of being obedient to God when our faith is tested remains with me to this day.

There's a framework God gives us in our walk with Him. It's different for each one of us. No matter how He lays it out in guiding us, it's important to work within His boundaries.

We may plan and labor and plan some more. We do all we can to meet our needs. But when we have exhausted our resources, we must remember the guidelines He has set for us. No matter what, we need to remember not to step outside His will. Somehow God gives us the shred of faith we desperately need at the time.

There is something far greater than our physical needs: the necessity of God's presence in our lives. When we do all we can to solve our problems and present our insufficiencies to Him, God takes over from there. The Lord knows what we need before we even ask. He has a better knowledge than we do ourselves.

The next time you are faced with a seemingly impossible situation, remember Aunt Virginia and Uncle Theodore's experience. Don't hesitate to ask God for His help. After you do, watch the amazing way He provides.

Through All the Changing Scenes of Life

Through all the changing scenes of life,
In trouble and in joy,
The praises of my God shall still
My heart and tongue employ.

O magnify the Lord with me,
With me exalt His name;
When in distress to Him I called,
He to my rescue came.

Fear Him, ye saints and you will then
Have nothing else to fear;
Make His service your delight;
Your wants shall be His care.

For God preserves the souls of those
Who on His truth depend;
To them and their posterity,
His blessing shall descend.

To Father, Son, and Holy Ghost,
The God whom we adore,
Be glory, as it was, is now,
And shall be evermore. Amen.

Nahum Tate, 1652–1715
and Nicholas Brady, 1659–1726

MY WANTS AND NEEDS ARE IN YOUR HANDS

You and I just made it through another tough time, Lord. Thank You for being with me every step of the way. I didn't expect financial disaster to strike like this. I felt like everything crumbled around me. In turn, my emotions went into turmoil. It seems there was no way to prepare for such a crisis.

Thank You for showing me the way to pare down my spending and teaching me how to eliminate some of the luxuries and credit payments. I'm grateful for Your making it possible for me not to take on more and more working hours, and having to miss time with my family. Thank You for being my problem solver in what seemed to be a hopeless situation.

I realize making careful and wise choices according to Your will brings a feeling of security and peace of mind. All the possessions I've longed for aren't nearly as important as putting my financial and emotional life in order.

After I did my best in adjusting my lifestyle to cope with this catastrophe, it seemed like help came out of thin air. Air, that is, from Your doing. I thank You for taking over and meeting my needs.

Thank You, Lord, for those who reached out

and helped me. Remind me, I pray, to be generous to others in return. Let my blessings scatter to those around me in need. Thank You for helping me keep my focus on You during the hard times. I praise You for how I was able to keep a steadfast heart and draw from Your wisdom and strength.

The next time disaster strikes, I will not fear. You are the triumph over my foes. Help me bear in mind how You remain with me and guide me through.

Teach me to yield my wants and needs to You, dear Lord. Whether I have much or little, let my wants comply to Your will.

My heart is fixed on You, dear Lord. How wonderful is the way You shower me with Your favor each time I submit to You. Thank You for anointing me with Your blessings over and over.

Even when I don't have many material possessions, I feel rich, for I am a child of You, my King. You know my needs and my heart's desires. You also know what is best for me. Thank You for being Lord over all.

Life in
Its Fullness

"I have come that they may have life,
and that they may have it more abundantly."

John 10:10 NKJV

I Am Following Jesus

Then he said to them all:
"If anyone would come after me,
he must deny himself and
take up his cross daily and follow me.
For whoever wants to save his life will lose it,
but whoever loses his life for me will save it."

Luke 9:23–24 niv

Brian was an average sixteen year old when he began attending our church. It wasn't long until he became a Christian. Because of his decision to follow the Lord, he glowed with a fresh, new enthusiasm every time he attended our youth Bible studies. In spite of his struggle to memorize the important Bible verses his youth leader encouraged him to learn, Brian beamed with excitement at how he now had Christian friends and a great new way of life.

Brian had a lot to learn. Every new Bible lesson made his eyes bulge with delight. He soaked up the words like a sponge.

During one of the Bible studies, his youth leader showed how the kids could resist temptation.

The leader explained the best way was to quote a Bible Scripture they had memorized, then turn their backs on sin and stay away from it. Brian listened intently.

The next time the group met, the young Christian told of his new experience. He felt like the devil had been trying to convince him he wasn't really a Christian, only playacting. He went on to share how he wrestled with that idea to the point of sleeplessness.

By the second night, Brian was fed up. His eyes snapped with satisfaction when he told the rest of the story. He described how he jumped out of bed, mumbling, "This is the last straw." He grabbed his Bible and rapidly opened it to John 3:16–18 (KJV).

He sat on the side of his bed and read the verses aloud. " 'For God so loved the world, that he gave his only begotten Son,' " he said confidently, " 'that whosoever believeth in him should not perish, but have everlasting life.' "

Brian went on, pointing his finger heavenward, wearing a determined look on his face.

" 'For God sent not his Son into the world to condemn the world; but that the world through him might be saved.

" 'He that believeth on him is not condemned: but he that believeth not is condemned already, because he hath not believed in the name of the only begotten Son of God.' "

Brian smiled at the group and pointed his thumb to his chest. "*I* am following Jesus!"

He described how he laid his open Bible on the nightstand and prayed to God for help, ending with a triumphant "Amen!" Then he announced in a firm voice, "Here it is, devil. Yes, I am saved by Jesus and I belong to Him. Read it for yourself and don't bug me anymore!"

Another smile lit up Brian's face when he explained how he felt a sudden peace, thanked God for victory, then rolled over and slept soundly.

* * *

Years have passed since Brian made his decision to follow Christ. He has experienced many ups and downs, along with great adventures in his walk with the Lord, especially the joy of his now being a youth leader.

Best of all, he has never stopped pointing his thumb to his chest while saying wholeheartedly again and again, "*I* am following Jesus!"

GOD'S POWER BY A RIVERBANK

"But blessed is the man who trusts in the LORD,
whose confidence is in him.
He will be like a tree planted by the water
that sends out its roots by the stream."

JEREMIAH 17:7–8 NIV

A hectic schedule had left me worn-out physically and mentally. Too many days began with my hasty prayers while I dashed out the door. I needed an escape, even if it could be a short one. I slipped on my sweats and tennis shoes, grabbed my Bible, and trudged to a nearby riverbank.

"I'm used up, Lord. Please refill me and bring back the joy and vitality I so desperately need from You."

My whispered prayer ascended above the rippling waters. I sank to my knees at the gnarled base of a huge maple tree. Its roots must have gone beneath the soil as deep as the tree was tall, drawing in water for strength and growth. I needed to tap my spiritual roots into the endless love and power of Jesus Christ.

Time no longer was an object. I opened my heart to God and listened to Him. He filled my soul as I read from His Word. He shared with me how as I draw from His strength, His marvelous unlimited resources cleanse and energize me.

Communication between God and me went back and forth. I felt His presence to be totally at home in my heart. Like the tree I knelt under, I sunk my roots down deep into the soil of His marvelous love, and I knew He understood my every concern and need.

His calming presence helped me to get just a glimpse of how long and wide and deep and high His wonderful love really is. No matter how hard I tried to measure that love, I realized I could never fully comprehend it, neither see its beginning nor end.

As I drank from His cleansing water, He refilled and restored my parched and wearied soul. I rose from my knees, replenished with God's power and love.

"Thank You, Lord," I prayed. "Please remain with me through my day. Let's talk more tonight when I kneel again by my bed."

EVER-LIVING LAUGHTER

A merry heart does good, like medicine,
But a broken spirit dries the bones.

PROVERBS 17:22 NKJV

There are many things we can do to improve our health: proper food and rest, plenty of exercise, regular checkups from our doctors, etc. One more essential thing I find is the medicine of laughter—a deep-down dose of ever-living laughter from the belly.

The Bible tells us: "A cheerful heart is a good medicine" (Proverbs 17:22 RSV); and "The joy of the LORD is your strength" (Nehemiah 8:10 NKJV).

Medical studies prove good old-fashioned belly laughs accomplish many things for our health. When we experience those subterranean laughs from within, we breathe deeply. We release adrenaline. We get additional oxygen to our body and our brain. In addition, we become more alert. A good, hearty laugh sends natural painkillers through our stressed-out beings. Perhaps that's what we need in order to help get rid of some of those "knot in the neck" headaches.

Did you know a few minutes of deep belly laughing is as good as time on a rowing machine? It burns calories, eases tension, calms emotions, and helps relationships.

On the day Bob and I were married, my future father-in-law drove me to the church to check on the catering equipment. He gave me some advice that has stayed with me for forty-two years.

"Always keep your sense of humor, Neat," he quipped. "It will carry you and your love for one another a long way.

"When I get in trouble with Ma," he said, "I stick my head in the door and ask if I can throw my hat in first. Ma and I both always burst out in laughter."

We live in a complex world. Things don't always go well. Life may not continually be happy for us, but it can still be filled with God's joy. Let's not dwell on the sadness and the negative, but think on good things.

For as he thinks in his heart,

so is he [or she].

Proverbs 23:7 NKJV

Whatever things are true, whatever things are noble,
whatever things are just, whatever things are pure,
whatever things are lovely,
whatever things are of good report,
if there is any virtue and if there is anything
praiseworthy—meditate on these things.
The things which you learned and received
and heard and saw in me, these do,
and the God of peace will be with you.

PHILIPPIANS 4:8–9 NKJV

Here are some ideas on how to keep God's joy and laughter in our lives.

1. Take a smile and pass it on. Frogs are my favorite little critters. They just look harmless and hold onto that funny grin, no matter what. Each time I see one, I can't help chuckling.

   I stenciled a shirt several years ago with a picture of a big, green, grinning frog. I named that frog TASAPIO. Then I added the words: "*T*ake *A* *S*mile *A*nd *P*ass *I*t *O*n." I wore the shirt to rags.

Tasapio's name stuck to another frog—this time, a ceramic one. Whenever I talk with my students or do guest speaking about a positive attitude, I show them Tasapio. Try it. It really works.

2. Curl up your face muscles. Medical research again shows when we put on a happy face (even when we feel down), it tells our brains to function more positively.
3. Enjoy good belly laughs. First-rate clean cartoons, movies, funny stories, and books are a great help to our feelings of well-being. Whenever I talk with my husband and family members, they almost always have funny things to share with me. My sons and daughters-in-law have ways of taking situations and transforming them into hysterical humor. Some of them make me double over with laughter. They often revitalize my day.
4. Look at things on the bright side. Researchers say it isn't what is happening that dictates our outlook. It's the way we view it. While telling about an event, mention the good things. Let the bad things go. When the car breaks down, think of the extra time we gain from not having to run around. When it rains,

open the window and smell the clean, fresh air.

5. Thank God for who you are. Let's not worry about whether someone else is thinner or fatter, younger or older than we are. Let's be thankful we are all God's children—children, by the way, of a King. He made us; He loves us for our personal strengths and weaknesses.
6. Make grape jelly. When someone passes us a sour-grapes attitude, let's not allow it to spoil our mind-set. Instead, let's take those sour grapes, add the gracious presence of the Lord, and stir them into sweet, delectable grape jelly.

   Remember: "A soft answer turns away wrath, but a harsh word stirs up anger" (Proverbs 15:1 NKJV).
7. Spread the joy. When we come onto a good thing to share, let's spread the joy. A note, phone call, E-mail, or kind word can change someone's entire day.

* * *

Ever-living joy and laughter in Christ
produces a victorious life,
everlasting and free.

Count Your Blessings

When upon life's billows you are tempest tossed,
When you are discouraged, thinking all is lost,
Count your many blessings, name them one
by one,
And it will surprise you what the Lord hath done.

Are you ever burdened with a load of care?
Does the cross seem heavy you are called to bear?
Count your many blessings, every doubt will fly,
And you will be singing as the days go by.

So, amid the conflict, whether great or small,
Do not be discouraged, God is over all;
Count your many blessings, angels will attend,
Help and comfort give you to your journey's end.

Count your blessings, name them one by one;
Count your blessings, see what God hath done.
Count your blessings, name them one by one,
And it will surprise you what the Lord hath done.

Johnson Oatman Jr., 1856–1922

God has put us here to make the world brighter, happier, and better by our lives, and by helping bear one another's burdens. Every one of us should study how he can be a blessing to others. Let us cheer up the discouraged. If the love of God beats in warm pulsations in our hearts, how easy it will be to win souls for Christ! I have known a whole family to be won to Christ by a smile. We must get the wrinkles out of our brows, and we must have smiling faces. The world is after the best thing, and we must show them that we have something better than they have.

DWIGHT L. MOODY, 1837–1899

HELP ME MAKE GRAPE JELLY

Rejoice in the Lord always.
Again I will say, rejoice!

PHILIPPIANS 4:4 NKJV

Father, when sour-grapes attitudes are passed my way, they make me grit my teeth, as does the taste of vinegar. Help me not to get caught up in this kind of downbeat mind-set. Remind me, instead, to fix my thoughts on You.

When someone passes me sour grapes, show me how, I pray, to stir those offensive little morsels into the pure, winning sweetness of Your love—and make grape jelly! Not the sickening, phony sweetness of this world, but the unselfish, thoughtful kind that comes from You.

No matter what happens during my day, remind me to live life in its fullness, as You intend. Teach me to pass on kindness and gentleness to others. Grant me the strength to do so through the power of Your love.

When troubles surround me, help me not to be anxious but submit everything to You in prayer. I know I am Your child. I will trust in You and give You thanks as You help me with each day. All I need to do is tell You my problems and ask for Your help and Your peace—that surpasses any understanding—to stay with me.

I am determined in Your strength that whatever I think on will be true, noble, just, pure, lovely, positive, and praiseworthy.

Thank You, Father, for showing me how to experience abundant life, and for teaching me how to make sour grapes into pure, sweet Holy Spirit-filled jelly.

Seek

God First

"But seek first the kingdom of God
and His righteousness,
and all these things shall be added to you.
Therefore do not worry about tomorrow,
for tomorrow will worry about its own things.
Sufficient for the day is its own trouble."

Matthew 6:33–34 NKJV

HEART FLIGHT WITH GOD

The days of the blameless are known to the LORD,
and their inheritance will endure forever.
In times of disaster they will not wither.

PSALM 37:18–19 NIV

I met a wonderful Christian family through my friend, Cindy, and her husband, Stu. A remarkable thing happened to Cindy's father, Bill Sr., her mother, Vivian, her brother, Bill Jr., and Bill Jr.'s wife, Darla.

In April 1986, the four were getting ready to fly in a small 172 Cessna with Bill Jr. as their pilot, from Bonners Ferry, Idaho, to Ellensburg, Washington. They planned to meet Cindy and Stu and other family members at about 8:00 A.M. From there, Vivian planned to ride with her family to Whidbey Island, where she would baby-sit her granddaughter.

Stu, Cindy, and their family were driving from the Seattle area to Ellensburg. When they arrived, however, the four family members flying in from Bonners Ferry hadn't yet come in. Stu and Cindy thought Bill Jr. might have taken off in their little plane later than usual.

After a couple of hours of waiting, Cindy called the Bonners Ferry airport and was told the plane had left on time. The Cessna should have been there well before 8:00 A.M. By this time, everyone was getting worried.

Cindy talked with the FAA at the Ellensburg airport. The plane hadn't arrived. Neither had there been any accidents reported. Again, Cindy called Bonners Ferry Airport and talked with a member of the FAA. Still, nothing had been seen or heard of the plane. Where were they?

The FAA didn't know Bill Jr. had flown a different route—over the Cascade Mountains—in spite of the fact that he didn't normally fly over the Cascades to the Seattle area during uncertain weather conditions, so the FFA flew over the area the four were thought to have traveled. They picked up a beeper signal coming from the mountains near Priest River in Sandpoint, Idaho.

Stu, Cindy, and family decided to head to Bonners Ferry. But Cindy had to make one more dreaded phone call before they left: to Darla's mother, Dee. Dee is an incredibly strong person. She told them not to worry but to drive safely.

Dee contacted her brother who was stationed at Fairchild Air Force Base in Spokane. Dee's brother immediately sprang into action. Members of the Civil Air Patrol at FAB were dispatched to the airport in Bonners Ferry. There, the Bonners Ferry Rescue Team united their efforts with the CAP to search for the plane. People from all over offered help and were praying. Unfortunately, the team couldn't see anything because of the cloud cover.

Stu, Cindy, and family stopped every few miles to call and check in. As they drove, the group began talking about the what-ifs. After they discussed the worst that could happen, they refused to harbor negative thoughts. They would trust in God for the best.

* * *

Bill Jr., his parents, and Darla left about 6:00 A.M. in the Cessna. He decided to fly over the mountains because it would be quicker. The weather was sunny with a few clouds but appeared nonthreatening. They headed west over Caribou Creek Canyon, a 6,000-foot peak, and on toward Harrison Lake.

Before long, they experienced up- and downdrafts. After encountering an updraft of about 800 to 1,000 feet, the little Cessna stopped flying and began to shake. Bill Jr. regained control of the plane and explained to the group they had a good flying attitude (the climb) and airspeed. Although the nose was up, they were losing altitude. They were suddenly being pulled down at an alarming rate. Bill Jr. tried frantically to pull the plane back up, with no success.

Down it plunged. A huge rock face whizzed by the right window, only about three feet away.

Seconds later, the Cessna plowed its way through snow and rocks. The landing gear and tail tore off. The plane catapulted, hurled ahead about 800 yards, impacted again, and skidded 1,200 feet in the snow. Since it was spring, the still-ample snow-pack provided a good cushion for the plane as it crashed. (If they had been flying ten feet higher, they would have missed the mountain. Two feet lower, they would have hit the mountain broadside.)

When they stopped, Bill Jr. saw the front of the plane had been torn off just on the outside of the instrument panel. A big tree stood six to eight feet away, directly in front of them.

Bill Jr. reached down and turned on the beeper to signal their location. Because of how badly damaged the plane was, Bill doubted if it would work.

He urgently began checking to see if everyone was all right. Darla, a bit shaken, was okay. When she stood up, her seat was still attached to her. The seat had torn completely loose from the plane. During the landing, something had hit Bill Sr. in the back. For awhile, he didn't respond when his son called his name; but he finally got his breath. It did not take long to discover he had broken some ribs.

Vivian couldn't move her legs. The bottom of the plane under her seat was gone. Her legs were stuck in the snow! Bill Jr. found something to dig Vivian's legs out. She was finally able to stand but could barely walk. One of her legs was badly hurt.

Because of a gas smell, they climbed out of the wreckage and unloaded the survival gear as quickly as possible. Everyone was dressed in spring clothing. They stood a distance from the wreckage, shivering from the cold. Stunned, arms around one another, they stared at what had been the little Cessna. Parts of it were scattered over a fifty-yard area.

Although the family had gone through this terrible thing, they knew God was with them. Reverently and thankfully, they lifted their hearts to God and sang, "Thank You, Lord, for saving our souls."

Not knowing if the beeper was working, Bill Sr. and his daughter-in-law, Darla, would attempt to hike out for help. Bill Jr. stayed with his mother.

Mother and son watched their two loved ones start down the mountain and disappear from sight.

Frigid winds lashed at Bill Jr. and Vivian, gouging sharp, icy fingers through the survivors' clothing. A small canyon lay about three hundred yards away. They could find more protection from the cold there and build a fire. Bill carried a survival kit in one hand and held on to his mother with the other. Since Vivian couldn't walk well, she suggested it would be easier to slide down the slopes into the canyon. The descent to the first level spot wasn't too bad. The second run proved to be much steeper. It sent Vivian painfully tumbling end over end, with her injured leg flopping. Finally, they reached the area, took shelter, and started a fire. They huddled around it, prayed, and sang hymns.

Vivian feared for her husband. He had lost one shoe in the accident, and he was walking with several socks pulled over his foot. Knowing Bill Sr.'s injuries, Vivian didn't see how her husband could make it down the mountain. She did the one thing she knew to do best—pray.

God ministered to Vivian's heart by assuring her He hadn't brought them through the crash to allow her husband and daughter-in-law to die. They *would* make it.

Afternoon approached. Clouds and fog rolled in. Bill Jr. and Vivian could hear and see helicopters circling off and on. Later, they discovered it was the Bonners Ferry Rescue Team. Bill had put a solar blanket in the clearing to help make their location more visible. He and Vivian didn't think anyone could see them from the air, however, because of the cloud cover. After awhile, the helicopters left.

Around 5:00 P.M. Bill and Vivian were sitting by the fire when they heard a distant "Hello–o–o." At first they thought it was their imagination.

Again, they heard the shout. This time Bill jumped up, ran to the clearing, and shouted back. After that, they heard more helicopters.

Seven o'clock came. So did darkness. Another helicopter drew closer. Bill and Vivian shouted for joy when they were finally able to spot the chopper and spinning blades. Spokane, Washington, HeartFlite Rescue Team had joined the search. They were able to land a short distance away.

Before long, Bill and Vivian were lifted out and transported to Bonners Ferry Hospital. Vivian had torn three major ligaments in her legs. She ended up having surgery. Bill was all right. Both were shaken, but happy to be alive. They prayed once again for the other two still remaining in the mountains. Each time Vivian began to worry, she felt God's assurance that everything would be all right. Again and again, Psalm 121:2 came to mind: "My help comes from the Lord, the Maker of heaven and earth" (NIV).

* * *

The rest of the family anxiously kept in touch with the sheriff by phone, still praying for the clouds to part. News came at last that the rescue team had found an opening in the clouds. They had managed to rescue Bill Jr. and Vivian. Mother and son were being transported to Bonners Ferry Hospital.

When Cindy, the family, and friends arrived at Bonners Ferry and were reunited with Bill Jr. and Vivian, they were overjoyed. Vivian glowed with the ecstasy of the Lord. Later the family found out the time Bill Jr. and Vivian were rescued was the same time the family had prayed and said they would trust God. At that point, everyone's faith grew stronger than ever that Bill Sr. and Darla would also be saved.

Before the rescue team could continue the search, the clouds rolled back in. Night was fast approaching. The search team would have to postpone their quest until morning. Bill Sr. and Darla would be forced to spend the night on the mountain.

* * *

Bill Sr. and Darla continued their hike down the mountain. Iced-over six-foot snowdrifts made walking extremely difficult and tiring. On and on they trudged, forced to wade through streams of melting snow.

Occasionally, they heard a helicopter overhead. They couldn't see it because of the clouds. Each time it flew over, their hopes soared. Each time it continued on, their hearts sank.

Darla was getting discouraged. She was so cold, she could hardly stand. All she wanted to do was sleep. She kept telling her father-in-law she was ready to simply give up and die. Bill, however, had a strong enough will for both of them. He refused to be defeated. He kept assuring Darla over and over that they would make it.

Bill Sr. had thought to take a brightly colored afghan with them before they left the plane. As darkness fell, they knew they would be forced to spend the night on the mountain. The blanket would provide some shelter and help keep them warm. But not warm enough. The hikers discovered a damaged tree, with a branch formed like a bench. Throughout the night, Bill and Darla took turns sandwiching each other between the tree and the bench. One person sat on the lap and in front of the other, sheltering and providing warmth. When the cold became unbearable, they switched places. At times they shivered so badly it made the tree shake. Amazingly, when they shook, it increased their blood circulation.

They struggled through the night, trying to stay awake. Darkness seemed to last forever. At daylight, they spread out the afghan on a visible flat area, in hopes the rescue team would be able to see it. At the same time, they tried to spot a logging road and find their way out. By now, they were three or four miles from the crash site.

At the crack of dawn, Bill and Darla heard

shouts coming from two different directions. Bonners Ferry Search and Rescue had dropped from helicopters into an area they thought Bill and Darla might be and were searching on foot. Along with medical supplies, the team carried rations, warm clothing for the two, and boots for Bill.

As soon as Bill and Darla heard the shouts, their energy quickened. Frantically, they began shouting in return. Back and forth, they called. Approximately twenty-one hours after the crash, father and daughter-in-law were finally found. Clouds cleared enough for the HeartFlite helicopter from Spokane to locate them. Unfortunately, there wasn't enough of an opening for the helicopter to land. Rescue nurses and chain saws were lowered.

The helicopter couldn't get close to the group. Bill, Darla, and the rescue team would have to retrace some of their steps through cold streams and icy snow back to where the chopper hovered. If the helicopter landed, it could have become wedged in the snow, unable to lift again.

Bill was so cold he could no longer walk. Quickly and skillfully, step by step, the nurses carried Bill on a gurney, like two angels from heaven. Darla walked closely by his side. Relief swept over Bill and Darla as they were lifted into the chopper and flown to Bonners Ferry Hospital.

Darla appeared to be doing well physically and was released from the hospital. Bill's chest had filled with fluid. Because of this and his broken ribs, he would have probably died in another thirty minutes, out in the elements. His body temperature was below 94 degrees.

He was moved to a hospital in Spokane. His lungs healed nicely. Huge blisters on his feet also healed. The doctors were surprised that although Bill lost all of his toenails, he didn't lose any toes. Vivian recuperated in Bonners Ferry Hospital. After she was released, Vivian and her family gathered in Spokane to be with Bill Sr. and Darla. The love and care from friends and family, young and old, quickened the healing process for everyone.

Experiences from the plane accident made a difference in every family member's life. Each person grew even stronger in his or her faith in the Lord.

Because of their heroic service, HeartFlite received the 1986 MBB Crew Extraordinaire Award in Washington, D.C., for the rescue.

Bill Sr. and Vivian had spent most of their married lives raising a Christian family. Their children accepted the Lord in their youth. The parents taught Sunday school classes for teenagers and children for many years. They still continue to do so.

Their family loves and serves the Lord and often shows kindness to those around them.

Although Bill Sr. and Vivian have followed the Lord for years, they feel more of a dependence on Him than ever.

They believe God rescued them for a reason. Now they feel an urgency to rescue as many youth as possible, helping them accept Christ as their Savior.

Throughout their lives, all they have wanted to do is show love to their Lord. Little did they realize God would shower His mercy upon them in quadruple measure.

Used by permission from
Bill Sr. and Vivian

Grow old along with me.
The best is yet to be;
the last of life, for which the first was made.
Our times are in His hands who saith,
"A whole I planned, youth shows but half.
Trust God; see all, nor be afraid."

Robert Browning, 1812–1889

Some of our experiences in life are dangerous physically, others spiritually. No doubt many of us have been blessed by God's rescuing hand more than once. Although we may have earned a few of His blessings, all of them are given by His gracious love.

How thankful we can be for those who risk their lives for others, especially for strangers. We can be grateful for the faithful, everyday loving prayer warriors who quietly care and love and give of themselves.

The graciousness and love God bestows on us is far greater than the good things we do. In spite of our good-hearted efforts, the only way we can gain His favor or our way to heaven is when we accept Him and actively acknowledge Him as our personal Savior and Lord.

He is the Creator of all. He is the One who placed within us the love and compassion we share with each other.

We don't understand or have control of our futures. But one thing we can know for sure is that God loves and cares for us. No matter what turn our lives take, we can seek Him. As we open our hearts, He can help us. The more we submit to His will, the more He is able to work through us. Each time He does, God blesses our lives beyond measure.

God Bless You!

"God bless you!" from the heart we sing,
God gives to ev'ryone His grace;
Till He on high His ransomed bring
To dwell with Him in endless peace.

God bless you on your pilgrim way,
Thro' storm and sunshine guiding still;
His presence guard you day by day,
And keep you safe from ev'ry ill.

God bless you in this world of strife,
When oft the soul would homeward fly,
And give the sweetness to your life,
Of waiting for the rest on high.

God bless you! and the patience give
To walk thro' life by Jesus' side;
For Him to bear, for Him to live,
And then with Him be glorified.

El Nathan, 1840–1901

You Are First and Last

"Listen to Me, O Jacob,
And Israel, My called:
I am He, I am the First,
I am also the Last.
Indeed My hand has laid the
foundation of the earth,
And My right hand has stretched out the heavens;
When I call to them,
They stand up together."

Isaiah 48:12–13 NKJV

As I look back upon my life, Father, I marvel at the mighty ways Your hand has been upon me. Before I was born, You formed me and watched over me. In my childhood, You were there. When I asked You into my heart, You blessed me. Through my bumpy teenage years, You rescued me from wrong circumstances. Now I am an adult. You still are with me, helping and guiding me all the way.

Though my life is changing all the time, I shall not fear. The past was in Your hands; so do I place the future. You are my Lord. You are my beginning, my present, my future, and my eternity.

When times are difficult and my soul feels dry, I know You are here—pouring out Your Holy Spirit upon me. When all is well, You still remain—counseling, leading me all the way.

Bestow Your call to not only use my life, Lord, but those of my offspring. Keep them close to You. Protect them from wrongdoing and harm. May they, too, glorify You. Teach them the marvelous lessons You show to me. Let them spring up like grass in the field—like sturdy poplar trees, growing by flowing streams.

I pray they will always say, "I belong to the Lord. He is my all in all."

You are the first and last in my life, Lord. Apart from You, there is no other. Your hand laid the foundations of the earth. You spread out the heavens. All Your creation is subject to bow down to You.

You are my Lord, my God. How I praise You for teaching me what is best for me. Day after day You direct me in which way I should go. If I stray, You help me back to the right path. When I pay attention to Your commands, You give me peace like a smoothly flowing river. Your righteousness is like the cleansing ocean spray.

You are everything to me, Lord. You shall always be first in my life.

God's Blessings Be upon You

May you lift your gaze to the heavens
and hunger for the Lord, your God.
May your help come from Him,
the Maker of all creation.

May He not let your feet slip
outside of His Holy ways.
May He keep you safe day and night,
for He never rests.

May He encompass you
as you go out and come in.
May the Lord be your shade by day
so the sun will not harm you.

May He be your shelter
when the moon shimmers by night.
May He protect you with His mighty hand
and watch over you—now and forevermore.
Amen.

OTHER BOOKS BY ANITA CORRINE DONIHUE

If you enjoyed *When God Calls Me Blessed* be sure to look for other books by Anita Corrine Donihue at your local Christian bookstore:

When I'm on My Knees
Anita's first book, focusing on prayer, has sold nearly a half-million copies.
ISBN 1-55748-976-9. . . . . $4.99

When I'm Praising God
Anita's sequel to *When I'm on My Knees,* promoting praise as the key to a fulfilling Christian life.
ISBN 1-57748-447-9. . . . . $4.99

When I'm in His Presence
Anita's third book, encouraging women to look for God's working in their everyday lives.
ISBN 1-57748-665-X $4.99

When God Sees Me Through
Anita's fourth book in the series, celebrating the Lord's faithfulness through every circumstance of our lives.
ISBN 1-57748-977-2. . . . . $4.99

When I Hear His Call
The fifth book in Anita's series, offering challenge and encouragement to listen for, then respond to, God's call.
ISBN 1-58660-279-9. . . . . $4.99

Available wherever books are sold.
Or order from:

Barbour Publishing, Inc.
P.O. Box 719
Uhrichsville, OH 44683
www.barbourbooks.com

If you order by mail, add $2.00 to your order for shipping.
Prices are subject to change without notice.